Tutti frutti

Italian Artisanal Jams, Marmalades and Preserves

Text
Francesca Maggio

Photos
Marco Arduino

SiME BOOKS

To my daughter Veronica

Content

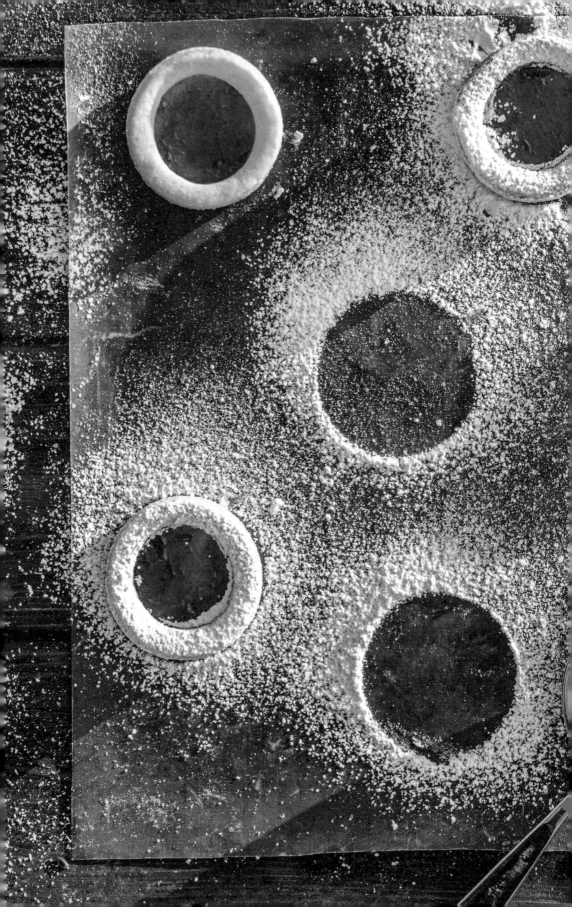

Introduction

Dreams always come true. You just have to believe in them.

I started writing this book during the first lockdown caused by the Covid-19 pandemic. Perhaps I chose the least suitable period to make a dream come true... But this time there was no excuse. I had a lot of time to work on my book, my first book.

In my family, fruit and vegetable preserves have always been homemade. I remember my mum and dad and I can see them again in my mind's eye in the kitchen with a large copper pot they called a *"quadara"*, with crates full vegetables to make the gianduja appetizer, with the tomato sauce, with eggplants in oil, with artichokes, as well as fruit juices and jams, which we called jams regardless of the fruit used to prepare them. So here we go: it is these jams that I will be telling you about.

The fruit that was used in our household was always too ripe. We always cooked up large quantities of preserves and the cooking went on for several hours. The jam was bottled, wrapped in woolen blankets and placed in large tubs, where it would remain until the jars were cold. The cellar held jam made five, six or more years earlier. When we went down to the cellar to fetch a jar, we always had to take the oldest one, regardless of taste.

My passion for cooking was likely passed on to me through my father. At a certain point, however, life introduced me to a sweeter world...pastry.

ICook, the cooking and pastry-making school which I founded and direct, allowed me to become friends with many pastry chefs. They really were the first people who supported me in my passion for the world of confectionery, a pastry sector often neglected, yet it is an important part of Italian confectionery culture and tradition.

The procedure to follow in making jams at home is the one familiar to our grandmothers, only with a few extra tricks made possible by better technology, by being able to use seasonal fruit, perfectly ripe, by the availability of fruits and spices that arrive from distant countries and the possibility to use a *refractometer*, an instrument that always ensures a constant density level in our products.

The recipes that I present in this book are all based on fruit, sugar and spices or natural flavors. I don't use any type of thickener or gelling agent, but I will write about them, albeit briefly.

All jams and marmalades can be personalized to suit your special needs or tastes. Remember that every implement you use will affect the consistency of your preparation.

You can also personalize the flavors with spices, roots, aromatic herbs, edible flowers and spirits. The important thing is not to overdo it, but always give fruit the leading role.

I am sure that by following my recipes you will succeed in preparing excellent fruit preserves and create new combinations with surprising colors and scents.

It only remains for me to wish you a delicious read!

Francesco Maggio

Valencia orange harvest in Lentini (Syracuse, Sicily). Right: cherries (Treviso, Veneto).

Prefaces

I met Francesca many years ago during one of my demonstrations. I remember that I immediately noticed her determination and confidence, which I then had the opportunity to see every time I met her in my courses. When she called me to become a teacher in her professional school, our relationship grew into mutual respect and a beautiful friendship.

One of her greatest passions has always been jams, candied fruit, jellies and marmalades, on which I have breakfasted a thousand times before starting a day full of courses. My favorite has always been her orange marmalade. I always kept my personal jar in the refrigerator and was very jealous of it. Needless to say, I also make orange marmalade, but hers is tastier!

When Francesca told me she meant to write a book all about jams, I was very happy. I remember I thought that she would finally receive great recognition for her lifelong passion and professionalism. Watching Francesca at work, when she produces jams, is an experience of unique and special beauty. Her gestures convey calm and confidence. Everything takes place with a precise logic.

Her methods are the result of years of work, tests and reasoning, of always being careful to keep to the path of tradition/innovation, but without getting lost by following the useless trends of the moment. Above all, she respects her ingredients and the seasonal nature of her produce.

Writing a book is a unique privilege. As I see it, it is like passing through customs to the eternity of our earthly passage, and will remain on some kitchen shelves for many years even after us. Writing a book is a wonderful act of love for our work. Seeing her commitment, sacrifices and products enclosed in its pages brings great fulfillment that I wish my dear friend may feel again and again.

I'm sure you will fall in love with her work because her first book could only be a concentrate of pure professionalism on this topic.

Here you will not find sterile recipes and summary procedures. These recipes have been studied, tried and tested many times and are explained clearly and exhaustively to enable readers to understand clearly how to make them.

Inside this book there are not only recipes, there is so much more. She herself is in here, with her passion, her determination, her heart and her great love.

Stefano Laghi

"Hello partner, would you like to write the introduction to my book?"

Yes, because Francesca still calls me that, even after some years, confirming the good relationship we have had during our careers. And how could I fail to be honored by her request?

Ours is the tale of a friendship and mutual professional esteem.

During our partnership, there has not been a day when we have not teased and provoked each other, because after all, Francesca and I have very similar characters.

Proud, precise, punctual in work commitments, touchy and passionate: these are just some of the adjectives that unite us, and you know, two identical characters are sure to quarrel frequently.

But if today we still call each other "partners", there must be a reason, right?

But let's get back to the book. I had been saying to Francesca for some time, why don't you write a book on the subject you excel in?

But you know the way Francesca is, she wants to do things properly, never haphazardly, and so she takes her time. She studies, experiments, tries, compares ideas with friends and colleagues, waits for the right season for this fruit to be at its finest and all this takes time.

But now she is ready, motivated more than ever, and has produced a work of art, a riot of techniques and colors.

Yes, because even for jams you need technical skills, knowledge, cleanliness and rigor.

All qualities Francesca possesses in abundance.

I had the privilege of previewing some of photos for this book and reading some of the recipes, and I can assure you that they will leave you more than content and satisfied.

I also had the good fortune to breakfast on Francesca's jams, on the morning before I started work at the Academy, and it has always been the best way to start the day.

And then if to the techniques and methods you add that touch of creativity and femininity as the topic chosen by Francesca for this volume, then here is a work that will go down in history.

Francesca, now remember, I am looking forward to receiving my copy, and this time you will sign it for me, and I am sure it will only be the start of your new adventure in publishing.

Luca Montersino

Finally Francesca has decided to write her book on Jams, which everyone was waiting for.

I was an iCook Academy trainer for 5 years and my best memories beyond training go back to the breakfasts prepared by Francesca. She always made sure I had orange juice, Greek strained yogurt, some sourdough bread and those delicious jams made by her. They were 15 minutes of pure happiness, the best way to start the day!

Before Francesca, my reference for jams was a Lady whom all professionals know: Christine Ferber, the famous Lady of Alsatian jams.

Today there is Francesca with her completely natural jams without the addition of pectin or other thickeners and gelling agents.

To write a good book you need three great skills: knowledge, technique and above all oodles of passion. All features that are part of this new book because Francesca has an almost intuitive understanding fruit. She always manages to keep their incredible colors as well as a balanced sweetness, never cloying and perfect gelation. But above all, she is ready to share this passion with real pleasure.

In this book, apart from talking about jams and marmalades, you will find a whole chapter dedicated to "candying". I am her biggest fan because I have never eaten candied oranges so good, moreover covered with dark chocolate. It's like touching heaven with one finger.

I am very honored to be able to write a few lines in this new book and I hope that, just like me, your mouth will water as you read it. Thank you, Francy!

Alexandre Bourdeaux

This book is a tribute to passion. The passion for making jams, marmalades, candied fruit and much more from the world of fruit... All in a completely natural way, without the addition of gelling agents, with only the natural pectin of apples. It is a truly admirable book, one of a kind, with few equals on the market and, in my opinion, chef Francesca is among the best at creating these delicacies we love so much.

Francesca's experience as a chef and teacher is fundamental to the innovation in each recipe in terms of taste and technique. In this book you will find unique preparations and flavors that will transport you back to your childhood. These extraordinary recipes, combined with the techniques used, confirm that success is achieved through hard work, discipline, and passion behind each creation.

This book will take us along a sweet path, learning from our wonderful chef. So, without further ado, I urge you to take delight in these recipes, which present precise instructions in a detailed and practical way. Finally, I would like to reiterate my admiration and respect for chef Francesca, inviting her to continue to inspire the new generation of pastry chefs around the world with her talent, and wishing her continued success in her professional life.

Antonio Bachour

Fattoria di Camporomano, Massarosa (Lucca, Tuscany).

Types of preserves

Marmalade is a preserve made with citrus fruits: orange, mandarin, tangerine, lemon, grapefruit, lime, citron, kumquat, bergamot.
Any preserve prepared with any other fruit is called *jam*.

Fruit compotes are pureed preserves, whose sugar content is lower than that of jams and marmalades. It is even possible to make compotes without adding sugar, using very ripe fruit. In this case, the fruit should be cooked only with lemon juice and natural flavorings or spices and then reduced to puree. Compotes can be stored in the refrigerator for a week, or longer, after pasteurization.

Fruit jellies are preserves made from fruit juice alone. Sugar is added in an equal proportion to that of fruit juice. To encourage the gel forming process, the fruit should not be too ripe and the peel is included. This guarantees a greater quantity of pectin.

Remember that the **quantity of fruit** that has to be contained in **100g (3½ oz) of final product** is established by law and varies according to each type of preserve:

- jam or marmalade must contain at least 35% fruit;
- chestnut cream must contain 38% fruit;
- extra-quality jam or marmalade must contain 45% fruit.

Fruit

The choice of fruit is fundamental in making preserves. It should be **seasonal**, if possible **organic**, perfectly fresh and at the right stage of ripeness. Unripe fruit contains few sugars, is too acid and lacks flavor, while overripe fruit contains little pectin and not enough acidity.

Citrus fruits in particular must be organic and not have been treated with diphenyl, a substance used as an anti-mold agent that ensures the fruit lasts longer on store shelves. Diphenyl is indicated by the European code E230.

Use all your senses in choosing the finest fruits. It is especially essential to smell and touch them to make sure they are at the right stage of ripeness.

Personally, I choose the fruit for my preserves strictly at farmers' markets. I inspect the market carefully before buying anything, to see who is offering the best fruit of the type I am interested in, not based on price but on quality.

After buying your fruit, first you need to **wash** it carefully to eliminate dust or any pesticides, then **trim** it to remove any damaged parts, **peel** it, if the recipe requires this, and pit stone fruit.

For fruit with a thin peel, such as peaches, I recommend blanching them for a few seconds in boiling water and then cooling them immediately in water and ice. This operation enables you to remove only the peel the fruit without removing the pulp. And in the case of peaches, you obtain fruit with a deeper and more brilliant color.

When slicing fruit, try to get pieces of **a uniform size** to ensure they cook evenly. To slice fruits like oranges, I recommend using a food processor to obtain thin slices all the same size.

You can also prepare your preserves with **frozen fruit,** provided you do not thaw it before preparation, to prevent the onset of oxidation.

In many recipes in this book, I have used specific varieties of fruit, choosing from those that in my experience have the most intense colors, aromas and flavors. If you choose these same varieties, you can also avoid adding spices or aromas because they are already perfectly sweet and fragrant without any additives. But if you can't find these specific varieties, don't worry. The result will still be great!

Wine-themed fresco in the Abbey of Novacella (Bolzano, Trentino-Alto Adige).

Spices

If it were up to me, I would add **vanilla**, **ginger** and **cardamom** to every jam. I love these aromas and they go well with almost every type of fruit.

I also really like some varieties of aromatic pepper, like the **Sichuan peppercorn**. Also known as "Chinese pepper", it is much less pungent than the pepper we all know and has a slight hint of lemon. The aroma of **long pepper** is also very pleasant. And it is unusual, being not ground but grated.

Equally fragrant is the **tonka bean**, a spice that should be used sparingly because it can be harmful in high doses.

Cinnamon and **star anise** remind me a lot of the warm family atmosphere of Christmas.

I often use also **edible flowers**, especially the buds of roses and lavender. To use them in preserves, make sure they are organic and dry.

Often, when bottling the jam into jars, I add the same spices that I used in cooking in the jars, for decoration but above all to intensify the aroma of the jam.

Sugars

In addition to sucrose, in jams and marmalades you can use other types of **natural sweeteners**: grape sugar, honey, cane sugar, raw sugar, fructose. Each of them has a different flavor and sweetening power.

Acids

The acids most used in the preparation of fruit compotes are **citric acid E330** and **lemon juice**. The latter is to be preferred if you want a "clean", natural product.

I suggest you always add the acid at the end of cooking to obtain more stable gelation, and a product with a more intense color and a fresher flavor.

Pectin

Pectin is a natural food additive extracted from fruit that acts as **thickener**, **gelling agent** and **stabilizer**. Pectin as a food additive is marked with the European code **E440**. Pectins are mainly used in the food industry and by professionals in the sector to ensure a standardized product in terms of consistency and spreadability.

There are different types of pectin, each of which allows you to obtain a product with different textures and gelations.

In jams and marmalades, **HM pectin** (with High Methoxyl content) is used. This pectin is active in acidic environments and with significant amounts of sugar. And it is not thermoreversible, meaning it cannot return to its initial state after being heated and thickened.

The recommended percentage of pectin to add varies **between 0.5 and 1.5% of the weight of fruit.** Pectin should be mixed with a small percentage of sugar (about 8-10% by weight of the fruit) and diluted in water (about 8-10% by weight of the fruit) with a blender, to avoid forming lumps.

To obtain correct gelation, pectin must be added towards the end of cooking time and then continue until the desired cooking point is reached.

There is no accurate way of calculating the exact quantity of pectin to add: each fruit at a certain point of ripeness is a case apart. The only certainty can be obtained by carrying out a test each time with a small quantity of fruit, and then getting a more precise balance.

You can also make preserves without adding pectin. In this case, the consistency of the final product will change depending on the amount of pectin naturally contained in the fruit.

The fruit that naturally contains the most pectin is **apple**. In particular, quince or slightly unripe apples like Granny Smiths are very rich in it.

Other fruits – citrus fruit, currants, gooseberries and plums – also contain high percentages of pectin. Conversely, strawberries, raspberries, pineapples, blackberries, cherries, blueberries and figs do not contain much.

Always bear in mind, however, that **the riper the fruit, the less pectin it contains**.

Apple juice

This recipe makes about 1 liter (2 pints) of apple juice

Ingredients
**1 liter (2 pints) of water
1 kg (35 oz) of Granny Smith apples**

Wash the apples and remove any bruised bits.

Cut them into quarters, and keep the core with the seeds.

Put them in a pan, add water and bring to the boil.

Cook over low heat for about 30 minutes.

Drain everything through a chinoise without crushing the fruit. Next, filter the juice obtained using an etamine towel (see page 29).

Allow the juice to cool, then let it sit in the refrigerator overnight. The next day, filter the juice again with the etamine towel, to eliminate any impurities deposited on the bottom while it was in the fridge.

Apple juice is very rich in natural pectin, and you can add it to all your jams.
The proportion of apple juice is 20-30% for every kilogram of fruit used.
Furthermore, apple juice is an excellent thirst-quenching drink that you can bottle and pasteurize on its own or with the addition of sugar, spices and aromas to taste.

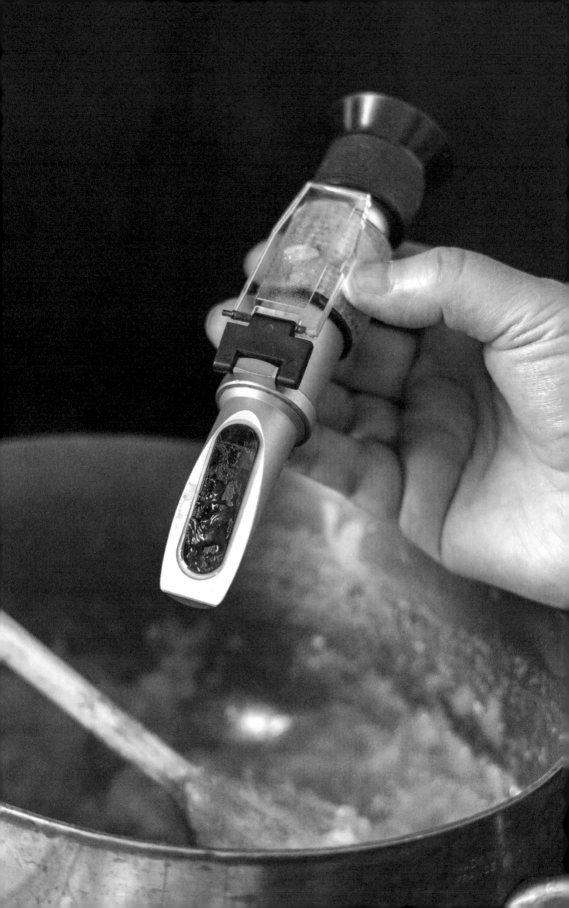

Equipment

The equipment needed to make jams and marmalades is easily found. Here is a list of everything you will need to prepare many delicious preserves.

- A **two-handled pan** for cooking, with a fairly large diameter, if possible, so as not to pile the fruit too high. But the pan should have sides high enough to avoid splashes. The best cooking material is non-tinned copper, because it conducts heat well. Steel is also fine and certainly easier to find in any kitchen;
- a **pan** for blanching fruit;
- a **chinoise**, also called a Chinese colander. This implement is perfect for separating fruit from juice. Otherwise you can use an ordinary colander with small holes instead;
- an **etamine fabric** made of fine-woven cotton. It is used to filter fruit juices and is essential in making jellies, which have to be perfectly free from fibers or filaments of fruit. If you don't have one or cannot get one, you can use a large sterile gauze;
- a **blender** or a **vegetable mill**, indispensable for obtaining uniform jams or marmalades, without any residual pieces of fruit. For red fruits I suggest using the vegetable mill, as the blender, due to its mechanical action, overheats the fruit and spoils its color;
- a **Microplane grater** for grate citrus peel. This tool has the particularity of not affecting the pith, the white part of citrus fruits which is often too bitter;
- **kitchen scales**;
- a **skimmer** to eliminate unwanted residues during cooking;
- a **kitchen robot** to cut fruit into very thin slices using the disks provided;
- a **potato peeler** to peel fruit without too much waste;
- a **paring knife** to clean fruit;
- a **carving knife**;
- a scrupulously clean **chopping board**;
- **wooden spoons**, new if possible;
- if the recipe calls for citrus fruit, an electric **juicer** to extract the juice without too much effort;
- **filters** or **fabric bags** for holding tea and spices, to preserve the cores and pips of apples or the seeds of citrus fruit, which are very rich in pectin.

The refractometer. Have you ever wondered why when you make the same jam from one year to the next you always get different results? There are endless variables involved (differences in the ripeness of the fruit, the amount used, and various other factors), but in particular it is the **correct cooking point** that ensures you get a preserve that is gelled but soft, which can be spread on a slice of bread without dripping or being too thick.

I'm sure you'll be thrilled to learn how to make your preserves with the same density from one year to the next.

To do this you will need a refractometer, an instrument that you may not have in the kitchen yet, but if you try it once, it will completely replace the old "saucer test" to check the cooking of your preserves. You can easily buy one on the internet for around 25-30 euros.

The refractometer measures the soluble solids in proportion to the liquids contained in the product. With it you can quite reliably determine the percentage of sugar contained in the fruit.

The **refractometer** has a scale that goes **from 0 to 90 degrees Brix**. 1 degree Brix corresponds to one part of solid substance in 100 parts of liquid.

Almost all jams and marmalades are cooked until they reach approximately **64°Brix**, that is, until the compound has 64% solids and 36% liquids.

To take a **reading**, put a drop of preserve on the refractometer slide. Make sure that the product is not hot. I recommend letting the preserve cool on a saucer before putting it on the glass slide.

Look inside the refractometer's eyepiece. The reading point is the number that can be read between the light area and the dark area of the scale.

You can also measure the temperature of your preserves with a **kitchen thermometer**. Indicatively, **64°Brix corresponds to 105°C (221°F)**.

The saucer test. If you do not have a refractometer or a kitchen thermometer, you can empirically check the correct cooking point of your preserves by performing a "saucer test".

This is very simple and easy to do in any kitchen. It does not call for special equipment. All you need is a saucer!

As you are making your fruit preserve, put the saucer in the freezer. In fact, to carry out the test properly, **the saucer has to be very cold**.

If you have the impression, as you stir the jam, that it has reached the right density, take a teaspoonful of it and place it, still piping hot, on the cold saucer.

Tilt the saucer and see what happens use the photo on the next page as a reference: if the jam flows easily, it's not ready (first saucer). So continue cooking and then repeat the test. But if the jam flows very slowly, it means that it is cooked to the right point and ready for bottling (second saucer). Finally, the third saucer shows a portion of preserve that has been cooked fot too long and has become excessively clotted.

Cooking tips

As for the cooking techniques for jams and preserves, there are many schools of thought, yet they really differ little from each other. Over the years I have experimented with a lot of them, so the advice I give you stems from experience. These tips will ensure you always get excellent results.

The first thing to avoid is to making too large quantities of fruit. The greater the quantity of the fruit, the longer it will take to cook. You might end up getting a jam that no longer has the freshness or color of fresh fruit.

My advice is to **use a maximum of 2 kg (4½ lb) of fruit at a time.**

Before cooking, put the fruit in a glass bowl with sugar and any spices or flavorings and leave it to soak for the time necessary for the sugar to begin to dissolve, then mix well and heat to its boiling point. You will see that the sugar will dissolve completely. Then allowing it to rest in the refrigerator will allow the sugar syrup to penetrate the fiber of the fruit, which will become shiny and soft.

At this point, let it soften for 12 hours in the refrigerator before cooking.

To get a clear, bright fruit preserve, it is essential to **constantly remove the froth during cooking.**

You will find that fruit will foam a lot when simmering, but there will be small patches of froth in some places, which you will have to remove. To do this, just hold a small bowl water and a skimmer near the pan. Whenever you remove the foam, put it in the bowl, making sure to change the water whenever it gets too cloudy.

Remember: don't skip this step. It is the most important one during cooking and it will make all the difference!

pH

The pH is an indicator that measures the **degree of acidity** of a substance on a scale ranging **from 0 to 14**.

A product can be acidic, basic or neutral, depending on its pH:

- it is **neutral** if the pH value is equal to 7;
- it is **basic** or alkaline if the pH is greater than 7;
- it is **acidic** if the pH is below 7;

So the lower the pH value, the higher the degree of acidity of a product.

Your preserves will be safe and protected from bacteria if their pH is below 4.

At home, pH can be measured with **litmus paper strips** that change color depending on the acidity of the substance. The measurement is carried out by immersing a piece of the paper in the jam, which will change the color of the paper according to its pH.

The litmus paper kit always contains a **color reference scale** to compare with your measurements. It will show you the pH value of your preserves quite reliably.

Remember that the substances the strips of litmus papers are made of could be toxic. So make the measurement separately on a small amount of preserve, to avoid contaminating it all.

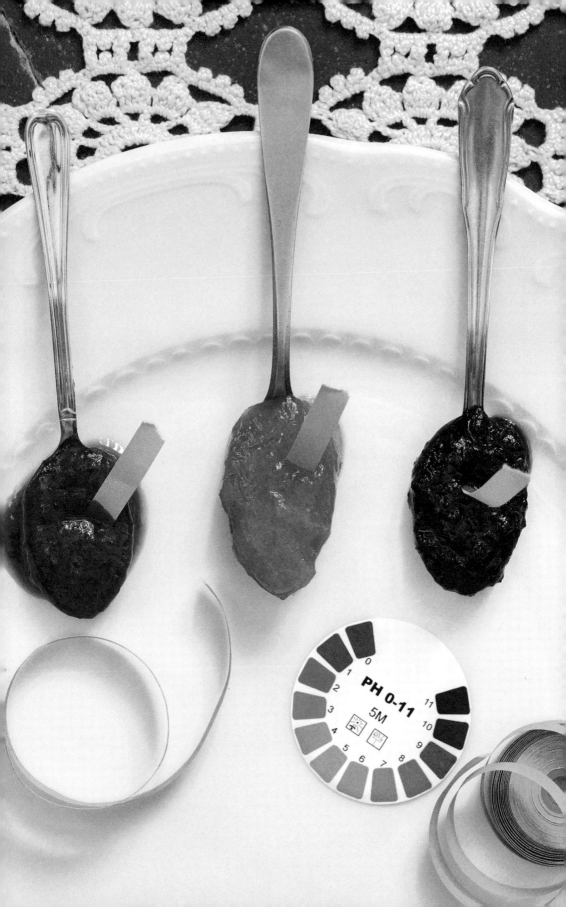

Jars

Glass is definitely the best material for storing your jams. It won't absorb odors, it can be sterilized and easily reused by washing in a dishwasher.

And being transparent, it allows you to quickly check the contents, without needing to open the jar.

You might want to choose glass jars with a **large mouth** to make them easier to fill.

Jars should have a **half-kilo (18 oz) maximum capacity**, to avoid keeping preserves open in the refrigerator for too long.

In my opinion, jars with **metal lids** are definitely the best. To ensure they are hermetically sealed and the product is safe, the lids must be new and replaced each time the jars are reused.

Bottling and ensuring jars are airtight

Special funnels for jams are commercially available. They are designed to be the right size and ensure you bottle preserves without spilling the jam.

Before bottling your jam, for added food safety I suggest you spray the jars with 95% alcohol.

As soon as the fruit preserve reaches the right density, pour it immediately into the jars, piping hot. At the time of bottling, the **jars** have to be kept at **a temperature as close as possible to that of the preserve**. To do this, I recommend that you keep the jars in the oven for an hour at a temperature of 100°C/212°F before use. In this way they will be sterilized and avoid thermal stress, which could cause cracks.

Don't fill the jars to the brim. Leave a space of **about one centimeter from the top**, which is essential to make them airtight.

Once the bottling is complete, if necessary, clean the neck of the jar with absorbent paper.

Seal the jars hermetically and leave them upside down for an hour. In this way, they will become **airtight**. To check that this has really happened, check that the metal lid has popped down.

After an hour, you should immerse the jars in a tub of cold water, to quickly lower the temperature of the preserve and keep its color.

Store your pots away **in a cool**, **dry place**, if possible **away from direct light**. The transparency of the glass jar would let in light, and it might modify the color of the product.

You can personalize your fruit preserves by adding a label to the jar with the name of the contents and the date it was made. Alternatively, you can write directly on the jar using a permanent marker. Personally, I prefer the second method because you avoid getting glue from the labels stuck to the jars. Later you can just use a metal scrubber to rub off the writing and your jars will be like new again.

Botulin

You have heard this mentioned endlessly.

Botulin (Clostridium botulinum) is a toxic anaerobic bacterium (thriving in oxygen-free environments) that can contaminate food and make it particularly dangerous to health.

The presence of botulin in preserved food can be easily recognized by the swelling the lid, the appearance of mold or the rancidity of the preserve.
Botulin is dangerous because it can proliferate while leaving the taste and aroma of the food unaltered.

In the case of jams and marmalades, the **large amounts of sugar** make the onset of botulism impossible.

Any preserve prepared with 1 kg (35 oz) of fruit and 600 g (21 oz) of sugar is safe because the high concentration of sugar prevents microorganisms from developing and guarantees the product's shelf life.
But a preserve prepared with 1 kg (35 oz) of fruit and 100 g (3½ oz) of sugar is not safe, because the sugar is insufficient to prevent the botulin from developing.

So a high quantity of sucrose is lethal to this bacterium, as is a sufficient degree of acidity.

Sterilization

Sterilization enables you to **destroy all kinds of microorganisms, including bacterial spores.**

Sterilization takes place in autoclaves through the action of superheated steam at temperatures greater than 100°C (212°F). In the food industry it is applied to products in which the proliferation of the bacterium that causes botulism is easier, especially canned food in oil.

Pasteurization

Pasteurization is a process which **reduces most of the microorganisms present in food** so that they do not pose a health risk. Unlike sterilization, this method has very little effect on bacterial spores, but is easier to perform in a regular home kitchen.

Personally, I have never pasteurized my jams. The high percentage of sugar I use in my recipes, hygienic rules for food processing, the correct cooking time and the right degree of acidity are sufficient to ensure they last one year and are safe to eat.
But I'll explain how to pasteurize, in case you decide to reduce the quantities of sugar or prepare large quantities of preserves.

Use a large pan and insert the jars filled with product well sealed. To prevent them from banging together as they boil, wrap them in kitchen towels.

Add water until the level covers the lids of the jars by a few centimeters.

The duration of the heat treatment depends on the size of the jars. Usually, jars for jams and marmalades have a capacity of no more than **250 g (9 oz)**, so **20 minutes** will be enough, starting from when the water boils.

To facilitate the removal of the jars immersed in the water, pots with special metal baskets can be found on the market.

It is important to know that ...

*   The factor that most influences the **preservation** of jams or marmalades is acidity and sugar content. The acidity of fruit, besides acting as a preservative, prevents sugar from crystallizing during cooking. Sugar plays an important part in the proper preservation of food products.

*   Another crucial factor is **cooking**. Overcooking could cause the sugar to crystallize, but undercooking could leave the product too liquid and easily attacked by molds and microorganisms.

    Almost all jams or marmalades reach the perfect consistency at 64°Brix. In some cases, however, you may have to reduce or extend the cooking time by bringing the finished product to a Brix degree greater or less than 64. This can be caused by several factors, above all the quantity of pectin contained in the fruit used and its point of ripeness.

*   In any case, before eating a preserve it is always good practice to inspect the jar to check that it is still airtight. Careful observation of the product and the experience you gain as you make more preserves will guarantee your food safety.

    Remember that it is preferable to consume your jams within one year from the date of preparation and that, once opened, the jars must be kept in the refrigerator and consumed within a week.

Calculating the concentration of fruit in jam
(Fruit used for 100g final product)

Stefano Laghi, pastry chef and a close friend, taught me how to calculate the amount of fruit present in 100 g/3½ oz final product. Thanks to this simple procedure you, too, will be able to calculate fairly reliably how much your jam will weigh after cooking.

Before making the calculations explained below, bear in mind that **the sugar present in fruit amounts to approximately 10% of its weight.**
The calculation will give you the weight that the full pan will have when your preserve has reached the right cooking point.
Just calculate the total weight of sugars, divide that number by the Brix degrees to be reached and multiply it by 100. To this result you will need to add the weight of the empty pan. From time to time during cooking, you will need to weigh the pan until it gets to the desired weight.
By using this method, it will be easy for you to calculate the amount of fruit to be used in your preparations.

Thank you so much, Stefano!

- **Fruit sugar = 10% of the initial fruit weight**
  Starting fruit weight = 1 kg/35 oz (1000 g/35 oz)
  10% of 1 kg/35 oz is 100 g/3½ oz. Therefore 1 kg/35 oz fruit contains 100 g/3½ oz. sugar.
- **Fruit sugar + sugar to add = total starting sugar**
  100 g/3½ oz (fruit sugar) + 500 g/18 oz (sugar to be added according to recipe) = 600 g/21 oz.
  The total starting sugar, therefore, is 600 g/21 oz.
- **Total starting sugar: 64 x 100 = weight of the jam obtained**
  Since we have to reach a sugar percentage of 64°Brix, we will make the following calculation:
  600 (total sugar): 64 (Brix) x 100 (fixed number) = 937.5
  Therefore 937.5 g/33 oz is the weight of the jam after cooking, once it has reached 64°Brix

- **Initial fruit weight in grams x 100: weight of the jam after cooking in grams**
  This last calculation will be used to check the quantity of fruit used for 100 g/3½ oz final product.
  1000 g/35 oz (fruit weight) x 100 (fixed number): 937.5/33 oz (jam weight) = 106.66 g/4 oz
  In this case, the weight of the fruit used per 100g/3½ oz final product is 106.66 g/4 oz.

Obviously, you can decide the sweetness of your preserves by increasing or decreasing the amount of sugar to suit your tastes and needs.

Be aware that according to European food regulations, marmalade/jam should contain a quantity of sugar equal to at least 45% of the weight of the fruit. If a product contains less sugar, it is called "compote", not marmalade/jam.

If you want to follow my recipes but with lower percentages of sugar, I suggest you always add pectin to avoid cooking the preserves for too long with consequent loss of taste, freshness and color of the fruit. My advice is that you pasteurize the jars for better food safety and longer shelf life (see page 41).

Labels for selling

If you intend to make labels for selling with all the information on the content of your products, always check the relevant laws for a labelling products that regulate your market.

As a rule, labels have to show:

- denomination: marmalade, jam, compote etc.
- ingredients
- sugar content per 100 g (3½ oz) product
- 'sugar-free', if this applies
- percentage of fruit used per 100 g (3½ oz) final product
- net quantity expressed in grams or kilograms, pounds or ounces
- best by date ("best by ...") or expiry date
- company name
- production site
- batch number of the product
- nutritional values
- methods of preservation

Jams and marmalades

Candonga strawberry and ginger jam

This recipe makes 3-4 250 g (9 oz) jars

Ingredients
1.2 kg (42 oz) Candonga strawberries
600 g (21 oz) sugar
30 g (1 oz) ginger root
40 ml (⅛ cup) lemon juice

Wash your strawberries, remove the stalk and any damaged parts, then cut them into pieces.

Put the fruit in a glass bowl, add the sugar and grated ginger. Mix well, then cover the container with cling film and leave it to soak until the sugar begins to dissolve.

Put it all in a pan on the hob and bring gently to the boil.

Then let the mixture cool and put it in the fridge, if possible in a glass bowl. Leave it to soften in a cool place for 12 hours.

Put the fruit back into a pan and bring it to the boil, skimming it as needed until the jam reaches the right density. You can check this with a refractometer (64°Brix), by using a thermometer (105°C/221°F) or doing the "saucer test" (see page 30).

When the density is right, add the lemon juice.

Fill the jars leaving a centimeter clear at the top, seal them hermetically and place them upside down for an hour, during which they will become airtight.

After an hour has passed, immerse the jars in a tub of cold water to quickly cool your jam and preserve the color.

Dry the jars carefully and, if you like, personalize them with lettering or a label before storing them in a cool, dry place.

The finest Italian strawberry is the Candonga cultivar. It is a juicy, flavorful variety grown in Basilicata. It has an elongated shape, with a bright red color and intense aroma, making it ideal for preparing excellent jams even without adding spices or flavorings.

Cherry, ginger and lemon jam

This recipe makes 3-4 250 g (9 oz) jars

Ingredients

1.2 kg (42 oz) cherries
500 g (17½ oz) sugar
zest of 2 lemons
20 g (7 oz) ginger root
300 ml (1¼ cups) apple juice
60 ml (2½ cups) lemon juice

Wash the cherries, remove the stalks and any damaged parts and the stones.

Put the fruit in a glass bowl, add the sugar, lemon zest and grated ginger. Mix well, then cover with cling film and leave it to soak until the sugar begins to dissolve.

Put it all in a pan on the hob and bring gently to the boil.

Then wait for the mixture to cool and put it in the fridge, if possible in a glass bowl. Leave it to soften in a cool place for 12 hours.

Arrange the fruit in a pan, add the apple juice and simmer, skimming when necessary until the jam has reached the right density. You can check this with a refractometer (64°Brix), by using a thermometer (105°C/221°F) or doing the "saucer test" (see page 30).

When the density is right, add the lemon juice.

Fill the jars to one centimeter from the top, seal them hermetically and place them upside down for an hour, during which they will become airtight.

After the hour has passed, immerse the jars in a tub of cold water to quickly cool the jam and preserve their color.

Dry the jars carefully and, if you like, personalize them with lettering or a label before storing them in a cool, dry place.

Black mulberry jam

This recipe makes 3-4 250 g (9 oz) jars

Ingredients

**1 kg (35 oz) black mulberries
600 g (21 oz) sugar
250 ml (1¼ cup) apple juice
40 ml (⅛ cup) lemon juice**

Wash the mulberries well, put them in a glass bowl and add the sugar. Mix well, then cover with plastic cling film and let the fruit soak until the sugar begins to dissolve.

Put it all in a pan on the hob and bring gently to the boil.

Then wait for the mixture to cool and put it in the fridge, if possible in a glass bowl. Leave it to soften in a cool place for 12 hours.

Process half of the mulberries in a food processor to partly remove seeds.

Put the fruit in a pan, add the apple juice and simmer, skimming when necessary, until the jam has reached the right density. You can check this with a refractometer (64°Brix), by using a thermometer (105°C/221°F) or doing the "saucer test" (see page 30).

When the density is right, add the lemon juice.

Fill the jars to one centimeter from the top, seal them hermetically and place them upside down for an hour, during which they will become airtight.

After the hour has passed, immerse your jars in a tub of cold water to quickly cool your jam and preserve its color.

Dry your jars well and, if you like, personalize them with lettering or a label before storing them in a cool, dry place.

The mulberry tree is recognizable by its fruits rather resembling blackberries. Ripe fruits may be white, black or red. They are soft, juicy, with a sweet and slightly sour taste. Widely used in Sicily in making ice cream and granita (slush), mulberries are also excellent for making delicious jams.

Ferrovia cherry and pine-nut jam

This recipe makes 3-4 250 g (9 oz) jars

Ingredients
1.2 kg (42 oz) Ferrovia cherries
300 g (10½ oz) Granny Smith apples
600 g (21 oz) sugar
300 ml apple juice
40 ml (⅛ cup) lemon juice
150 g (5¼ oz) toasted pine-nuts

Wash the cherries, remove the stalks and any damaged parts and the stones.

Peel the apples, core and then dice them.

Put the fruit in a glass bowl and add the sugar. Mix well, then cover the container with cling film and leave it to soak until the sugar begins to dissolve.

Pour everything into a pan on the hob and bring gently to the boil.

Then wait for the mixture to cool and put it in the fridge, if possible in a glass bowl. Leave it to soften in a cool place for 12 hours.

Put the fruit into a pan, add the apple juice and simmer, skimming when necessary until the jam has reached the right density. You can check this with a refractometer (64°Brix), by using a thermometer (105°C/221°F) or doing the "saucer test" (see page 30).

When the density is right, add the lemon juice and toasted pine nuts.

Fill the jars to one centimeter from the top, seal them hermetically and place them upside down for an hour, when they will become airtight.

After the hour has passed, immerse the jars in a tub of cold water to quickly cool the jam and preserve their color.

Dry the jars carefully and, if you like, personalize them with lettering or a label before storing them in a cool, dry place.

Ferrovia cherry is a variety from Puglia, certainly the best known and most widely exported worldwide. It has an intense dark red color and its shape resembles a heart. It is the ideal ingredient for delicious fruit preserves because it is juicy, sweet and crunchy.

Mixed berry and tonka bean jam

This recipe makes 3-4 250 g (9 oz) jars

Ingredients

**600 g (21 oz) raspberries passed through a vegetable mill and sieved
500 g (17½ oz) strawberries
250 g (8¾ oz) blackberries
250 g (8¾ oz) blueberries
1 kg (35 oz) sugar
½ tonka bean
60 m (¼ cup) lemon juice**

Wash the fruit thoroughly, remove any damaged bits and cut the strawberries in half.

Put the fruit in a glass bowl, add the raspberry puree, sugar and grated tonka bean. Mix well, then cover with cling film and leave it to soak until the sugar begins to dissolve.

Put it all in a pan on the hob and bring gently to the boil.

Then wait for the mixture to cool and put it in the fridge, if possible in a glass bowl. Leave it to soften in a cool place for 12 hours.

Arrange the fruit in a pan and simmer, skimming when necessary until the jam has reached the right density. You can check this with a refractometer (64°Brix), by using a thermometer (105°C/221°F) or doing the "saucer test" (see page 30).

When the density is right, add the lemon juice.

Fill the jars to one centimeter from the top, seal them hermetically and place them upside down for an hour, during which the vacuum will form.

After the time has passed, immerse your jars in a tub of cold water to quickly cool your jam and preserve its color.

Dry your jars well and, if you like, personalize them with lettering or a label before storing them in a cool, dry place.

Flat peach and vanilla jam

This recipe makes 3-4 250 g (9 oz) jars

Ingredients
1.3 kg (46 oz) flat peaches
500 g (18 oz) sugar
1 vanilla bean
40 ml (⅛ cup) lemon juice

Wash the peaches, scald them for a minute in boiling water and leave them to cool in water and ice.

Peel them, remove the stones and any bruised parts and dice them.

Put the fruit in a glass bowl, add the sugar and the vanilla bean cut in half. Mix well, then cover with cling film and leave it to soak until the sugar begins to dissolve.

Put it all in a pan, place it on the hob and bring gently to the boil.

Then wait for the mixture to cool and put it in the fridge, if possible in a glass bowl. Leave it to soften in a cool place for 12 hours.

Put the fruit in a pan again and simmer, skimming when necessary until the jam has reached the right density. You can check this with a refractometer (64°Brix), by using a thermometer (105°C/221°F) or doing the "saucer test" (see page 30).

When the density is right, add the lemon juice.

Fill the jars to one centimeter from the top, close them hermetically and place them upside down for an hour, during which they will become airtight.

After the hour has passed, immerse your jars in a tub of cold water to quickly cool your jam and preserve its color.

Dry the jars carefully and, if you like, personalize them with lettering or a label before storing them in a cool, dry place.

The flat peach, also known as Saturn peach, is easily recognizable from other peach varieties due to its flat shape, unmistakable scent and sweetness. The pulp may be yellow or white. This variety is excellent for making delicious fruit juices, compotes and jams. It is grown in various Italian regions.

Pellecchiella apricot and cardamom jam

This recipe makes 3-4 250 g (9 oz) jars

Ingredients

1.3 kg (46 oz) Pellecchiella apricots
600 g (21 oz) sugar
10 cardamom pods
60 m (¼ cup) lemon juice

Wash the apricots, remove the stones and any bruised parts and cut them in half.

Put the fruit in a glass bowl, add the sugar and the seeds from the cardamom pods. Mix well, then cover with cling film and leave it to soak until the sugar begins to dissolve.

Put everything into a pan on the hob and bring gently to the boil.

Then wait for the mixture to cool and put it in the fridge, if possible in a glass bowl. Leave it to soften in a cool place for 12 hours.

Put the fruit in a pan and simmer, skimming when necessary, until the jam has reached the right density. You can check this with a refractometer (64°Brix), by using a thermometer (105°C/221°F) or doing the "saucer test" (see page 30).

When the density is right, add the lemon juice.

Fill the jars to one centimeter from the top, seal them hermetically and place them upside down for an hour, during which they will become airtight.

After the hour has passed, immerse your jars in a tub of cold water to quickly cool your jam and preserve its color.

Dry your jars well and, if you like, personalize them with lettering or a label before storing them in a cool, dry place.

The Pellecchiella apricot is an heirloom fruit, an exceptional variety from Campania. Unlike other varieties of apricot, the pulp is very sweet and low in acid, ideal for being candied or made into delicious jam.

Ramasin plum and cinnamon jam

This recipe makes 3-4 250 g (9 oz) jars

Ingredients

1.2 kg (42 oz) Ramasin plums
600 g (21 oz) sugar
1.5 g (¼ teaspoon) ground cinnamon
30 ml (⅛ cup) lemon juice

Wash the plums, remove the stones and any damaged parts and cut the plums in half.

Put the fruit in a glass bowl, add the sugar and cinnamon. Mix well, then cover with cling film and leave it to soak until the sugar begins to dissolve.

Put it all in a pan on the hob and bring gently to the boil.

Then wait for the mixture to cool and put it in the fridge, if possible in a glass bowl. Leave it to soften in a cool place for 12 hours.

Put the fruit in a pan and simmer, skimming when necessary, until the jam has reached the right density. You can check this with a refractometer (64°Brix), by using a thermometer (105°C/221°F) or doing the "saucer test" (see page 30).

When the density is right, add the lemon juice.

Fill the jars to one centimeter from the top, seal them hermetically and place them upside down for an hour, during which they will become airtight.

After the hour has passed, immerse your jars in a tub of cold water to quickly cool the jam and preserve their color.

Dry the jars carefully and, if you want, personalize them with lettering or a label before storing them in a cool, dry place.

Ramasin is a variety of plum typical of Piedmont. These small fruits are a beautiful deep purple color. The pulp is soft and sweet and lends itself well to being made into compote, jam or delicious fruit in syrup.

Santa Clara plum jam with vanilla and rum

This recipe makes 3-4 250 g (9 oz) jars

Ingredients
1.3 kg (46 oz) Santa Clara plums
600 g (21 oz) sugar
1 vanilla bean
40 ml (⅛ cup) lemon juice
40 ml (⅛ cup) rum

Wash the plums, remove the stones and any damaged parts and cut them in half.

Put the fruit in a glass bowl, add the sugar and the vanilla bean cut in half. Mix well, then cover with cling film and leave it to soak until the sugar begins to dissolve.

Put it all in a pan, place it on the hob and bring gently to the boil.

Then wait for the mixture to cool and put it in the fridge, if possible in a glass bowl. Leave it to soften in a cool place for 12 hours.

Put the fruit back in a pan and simmer, skimming when necessary until the jam has reached the right density. You can check this with a refractometer (64°Brix), by using a thermometer (105°C/221°F) or doing the "saucer test" (see page 30).

When the density is right, add the lemon juice and rum.

Fill the jars to one centimeter from the top, seal them hermetically and place them upside down for an hour, during which they will become airtight.

After the hour has passed, immerse your jars in a tub of cold water to quickly cool your jam and preserve its color.

Dry the jars carefully and, if you like, personalize them with lettering or a label before storing them in a cool, dry place.

Santa Clara plums, widely grown in the Saluzzo area of Piedmont, are quite large fruits, purple in color, with a fairly sweet pulp. This variety is excellent for making into syrup and jam.

Peach and chocolate jam

This recipe makes 3-4 250 g (9 oz) jars

Ingredients

1.3 kg (46 oz) peaches
500 g (17½ oz) sugar
1 vanilla bean
30 ml (⅛ cup) lemon juice
30 ml (⅛ cup) Amaretto di Saronno liqueur
50 g (1¾ oz) dark chocolate

Wash the peaches, scald them for a minute in boiling water and leave them to cool in water and ice.

Peel them, remove the stones and any bruised parts and dice them.

Put the fruit in a glass bowl, add sugar and the vanilla bean cut in half.

Mix well, then cover with cling film and leave it to soak until the sugar begins to dissolve.

Put it all in a pan, place it on the hob and bring gently to the boil.

Then wait for the mixture to cool and put it in the fridge, if possible in a glass bowl. Leave it to soften in a cool place for 12 hours.

Put the fruit in a pan again and simmer, skimming it when necessary until the jam has reached the right density. You can check this with a refractometer (64°Brix), by using a thermometer (105°C/221°F) or doing the "saucer test" (see page 30).

When the density is right, add the lemon juice, Amaretto di Saronno and chocolate shavings.

Fill the jars to one centimeter from the top, close them hermetically and place them upside down for an hour, during which they will become airtight.

After the hour has passed, immerse your jars in a tub of cold water to quickly cool your jam and preserve its color.

Dry the jars carefully and, if you like, personalize them with lettering or a label before storing them in a cool, dry place.

Red currant jam

This recipe makes 3-4 250g (9 oz) jars

Ingredients
1.1 kg (35 oz) red currants
600 g (21 oz) sugar
30 ml (⅛ cup) lemon juice

Wash the currants well, use a fork to detach the berries from the stems and remove any damaged parts.

Put the fruit in a glass bowl and add the sugar.

Mix well, then cover with cling film and leave it to soak until the sugar begins to dissolve.

Put it all in a pan, place it on the hob and bring gently to the boil.

Then wait for the mixture to cool and put it in the fridge, if possible in a glass bowl. Leave it to soften in a cool place for 12 hours.

Process half of the currants in a food processor to partly remove seeds.

Put the fruit in a pan again and simmer, skimming it when necessary, until the jam has reached the right density. You can check this with a refractometer (64°Brix), by using a thermometer (105°C/221°F) or doing the "saucer test" (see page 30).

When the density is right, add the lemon juice.

Fill the jars to one centimeter from the top, seal them hermetically and place them upside down for an hour, during which they will become airtight.

After the hour has passed, immerse your jars in a tub of cold water to quickly cool your jam and preserve its color.

Dry the jars carefully and, if you like, personalize them with lettering or a label before storing them in a cool, dry place.

Peach and pear jam with Moscato and lavender

This recipe makes 3-4
250 g (9 oz) jars

Ingredients

650 g (23 oz) peaches
650 g (23 oz) pears
600 g (21 oz) sugar
100 ml (½ cup) Moscato wine
grated zest of 1 lemon
1 tablespoon of organic dried lavender flowers
40 ml (⅛ cup) lemon juice

Wash the peaches, scald them for a minute in boiling water and leave them to cool in water and ice.

Peel them, remove the stones and any bruised parts, and dice them.

Peel the pears, core and dice them.

Put the fruit in a glass bowl, add sugar, Moscato, lemon zest and the lavender flowers placed in a sachet.

Mix well, then cover with cling film and leave to soak until the sugar begins to dissolve.

Put it all in a pan on the hob and bring gently to the boil.

Then wait for the mixture to cool and put it in the fridge, if possible in a glass bowl. Leave it to soften in a cool place for 12 hours.

Put the fruit in a pan again and simmer, skimming it when necessary, until the jam has reached the right density. You can check this with a refractometer (64°Brix), by using a thermometer (105°C/221°F) or doing the "saucer test" (see page 30).

When the density is right, remove the sachet with lavender and add the lemon juice.

Fill the jars to one centimeter from the top, seal them hermetically and place them upside down for an hour, during which they will become airtight.

After the hour has passed, immerse your jars in a tub of cold water to quickly cool your jam and preserve its color.

Dry the jars carefully and, if you like, personalize them with lettering or a label before storing them in a cool, dry place.

Dottato fig, honey and vanilla jam

This recipe makes 3-4 250 g (9 oz) jars

Ingredients

1 kg (35 oz) Dottato figs
400 g (14 oz) sugar
100 g (3½ oz) acacia honey
2 vanilla pods
40 ml (⅛ cup) lemon juice
grated zest of 1 lemon

Wash the figs, dry them, remove the stalk and cut them into four parts.

Put the fruit in a glass bowl and add the sugar, honey, vanilla pods cut in half and lemon zest.

Mix well, then cover with cling film and leave the ingredients to soak until the sugar begins to dissolve.

Put everything in a pan, place it on the hob and bring gently to the boil.

Then wait for the mixture to cool and put it in the fridge, if possible in a glass bowl. Leave it to soften in a cool place for 12 hours.

Put the fruit in a pan again and simmer, skimming when necessary, until the jam has reached the right density. You can check this with a refractometer (64°Brix), by using a thermometer (105°C/221°F) or doing the "saucer test" (see page 30).

When the density is right, add the lemon juice.

Fill the jars to one centimeter from the top, seal them hermetically and place them upside down for an hour, during which they will become airtight.

After the hour has passed, immerse your jars in a tub of cold water to quickly cool your jam and preserve its color.

Dry the jars carefully and, if you like, personalize them with lettering or a label before storing them in a cool, dry place.

Dottato figs (sometimes called Kadota figs) are one of the most prized varieties in Italy. With a honeyed flavor, they are particularly small and soft, ideal for drying, and for making compotes, jams and delicious caramelized morsels to be served with cheeses.

Peach, nectarine and apricot jam with lavender flowers

This recipe makes 3-4
250 g (9 oz) jars

Ingredients
650 g (23 oz) nectarines
650 g (23 oz) apricots
600 g (21 oz) sugar
1 tablespoon organic
dried lavender flowers
40 ml (⅛ cup) lemon juice

Wash the peaches, scald them for a minute in boiling water and leave them to cool in water and ice. Peel them, remove the stones and any bruised parts and dice them. Wash the apricots, cut them in half and remove the stones.

Put the fruit in a glass bowl, add the sugar and the lavender enclosed in a muslin sachet. Mix well, then cover with cling film and leave it to soak until the sugar begins to dissolve.

Put it all in a pan, place it on the hob and bring gently to the boil.

Then wait for the mixture to cool and put it in the fridge, if possible in a glass bowl. Leave it to soften in a cool place for 12 hours.

Put the fruit in a pan again and simmer, skimming when necessary until the jam has reached the right density. You can check this with a refractometer (64°Brix), by using a thermometer (105°C/221°F) or doing the "saucer test" (see page 30).

When the density is right, remove the sachet of lavender and add the lemon juice.

Fill the jars to one centimeter from the top, seal them hermetically and place them upside down for an hour, during which they will become airtight.

After the hour has passed, immerse your jars in a tub of cold water to quickly cool your jam and preserve its color.

Dry the jars carefully and, if you like, personalize them with lettering or a label before storing them in a cool, dry place.

Nectarines are grown in areas with a mild climate. The major nectarine producing regions in Italy are the Veneto, Emilia Romagna, Lazio and Campania. The main feature of this peach variety is the absence of fuzz on the skin. The fruits are sweet and perfect for making delicious jams or preserving in syrup.

Raspberry and star anise jam

This recipe makes 3-4 250 g (9 oz) jars

Ingredients

1.5 kg (53 oz) raspberries
600 g (21 oz) sugar
1 star anise pod
40 ml (⅛ cup) lemon juice

Wash the raspberries well and remove any damaged parts.

Put the fruit in a glass bowl, add the sugar and the star anise.

Mix everything, cover with cling film and leave it to soak until the sugar begins to dissolve.

Put it all in a pan, place it on the hob and bring gently to the boil.

Then wait for the mixture to cool and put it in the fridge, if possible in a glass bowl. Leave it to soften in a cool place for 12 hours.

Process half of the raspberries in a food processor to partly remove seeds.

Put the fruit in a pan and simmer, skimming it when necessary until the jam has reached the right density. You can check this with a refractometer (64°Brix), by using a thermometer (105°C/221°F) or doing the "saucer test" (see page 30).

When the density is right, add the lemon juice.

Fill the jars to one centimeter from the top, seal them hermetically and place them upside down for an hour, during which they will become airtight.

After the hour has passed, immerse your jars in a tub of cold water to quickly cool your jam and preserve its color.

Dry the jars carefully and, if you like, personalize them with lettering or a label before storing them in a cool, dry place.

Oxheart tomato jam with aromatic herbs and rum

This recipe makes 3-4 250 g (9 oz) jars

Ingredients

1.3 kg (46 oz) oxheart tomatoes
500 g (17½ oz) sugar
zest of 1 lemon
1 sprig of Greek basil
4-5 leaves of lemon verbena
30 ml (⅛ cup) lemon juice
30 ml (⅛ cup) rum

Wash the tomatoes, scald them for a minute in boiling water and leave them to cool in water and ice.

Peel them, remove the seeds and any damaged parts and dice them.

Place them in a glass bowl, add sugar, lemon zest and the aromatic herbs.

Mix well, then cover with cling film and leave them to soak until the sugar begins to dissolve.

Put everything in a pan, place it on the hob and bring it gently to the boil.

Then wait for the mixture to cool and put it in the fridge, if possible in a glass bowl. Leave it to soften in a cool place for 12 hours.

Put the tomatoes in a pan again and simmer, skimming when necessary, until the jam has reached the right density. You can check this with a refractometer (64°Brix), by using a thermometer (105°C/221°F) or doing the "saucer test" (see page 30).

When the density is right, add the lemon juice and rum.

Fill the jars to one centimeter from the top, seal them hermetically and place them upside down for an hour, during which they will become airtight.

After the hour has passed, immerse your jars in a tub of cold water to quickly cool your jam and preserve its color.

Dry the jars carefully and, if you like, personalize them with lettering or a label before storing them in a cool, dry place.

Wild blueberry and rum jam

This recipe makes 3-4 250 g (9 oz) jars

Ingredients

1 kg (35 oz) wild mountain blueberries
600 g (21 oz) sugar
zest of 2 lemons
200 ml (¾ cup) apple juice
40 ml (⅛ cup) lemon juice
40 ml (⅛ cup) rum

Wash the blueberries well and check that they are all intact.

Put the fruit in a glass bowl, add the sugar and lemon zest.

Mix well, then cover with cling film and leave it to soak until the sugar begins to dissolve.

Put it all in a pan, place it on the hob and bring gently to the boil.

Then wait for the mixture to cool and put it in the fridge, if possible in a glass bowl. Leave it to soften in a cool place for 12 hours.

Put the fruit in a pan again, add the apple juice and simmer, skimming when necessary, until the jam has reached the right density. You can check this with a refractometer (64°Brix), by using a thermometer (105°C/221°F) or doing the "saucer test" (see page 30).

When the density is right, add the lemon juice and rum.

Fill the jars to one centimeter from at the top, seal them hermetically and place them upside down for an hour, during which they will become airtight.

After the hour has passed, immerse your jars in a tub of cold water to quickly cool your jam and preserve its color.

Dry the jars carefully and, if you like, personalize them with lettering or a label before storing them in a cool, dry place.

Marsh birches and blueberry bushes. Left: blueberries from Alpe Campra (Verbano-Cusio-Ossola, Piedmont)

Williams pear, chocolate and tonka bean jam

This recipe makes 3-4 250 g (9 oz) jars

Ingredients

1.3 kg (46 oz) Williams pears
600 g (21 oz) sugar
½ tonka bean
30 ml (⅛ cup) lemon juice
150 g (5¼ oz) dark chocolate

Wash the pears well, peel them, remove any bruised parts and dice them.

Put the fruit in a glass bowl and add the sugar and a grated tonka bean.

Mix well, then cover with cling film and leave it to soak until the sugar begins to dissolve.

Put it all in a pan, place it on the hob and bring gently to the boil.

Then wait for the mixture to cool and put it in the fridge, if possible in a glass bowl. Leave it to soften in a cool place for 12 hours.

Put the fruit in a pan again and simmer, skimming it when necessary, until the jam has reached the right density. You can check this with a refractometer (64°Brix), by using a thermometer (105°C/221°F) or doing the "saucer test" (see page 30).

When the density is right, add the lemon juice and chocolate shavings.

Fill the jars to one centimeter from the top, seal them hermetically and place them upside down for an hour, during which they will become airtight.

After the hour has passed, immerse your jars in a tub of cold water to quickly cool your jam and preserve its color.

Dry the jars carefully and, if you like, personalize them with lettering or a label before storing them in a cool, dry place.

The Williams pear (called the Bartlett pear in the United States) is a variety of English origin, well known and common in Italy. The pulp is white, fragrant, soft, sweet and juicy, perfect for making jam and delicious fruit juices.

Williams pear, dried fig, almond and rum jam

This recipe makes 3-4
250 g (9 oz) jars

Ingredients

1.3 kg (46 oz) Williams pears
450 g (16 oz) sugar
125 g (4½ oz) dried figs
50 g (1¾ oz) rum
35 ml (6 teaspoons) lemon juice
50 g (1¾ oz) toasted flaked almonds

Wash the pears well, peel them, remove any damaged parts and dice them.

Put the fruit in a glass bowl and add the sugar.

Mix well, then cover with cling film and leave it to soak until the sugar begins to dissolve.

Put it all in a pan, place it on the hob and bring gently to the boil.

Then wait for the mixture to cool and put it in the fridge, if possible in a glass bowl. Leave it to soften in a cool place for 12 hours.

Meanwhile, slice the dried figs finely and soak them in rum overnight.

Put all the fruit in a pan, add the dried figs with rum and simmer, skimming when necessary, until the jam has reached the right density. You can check this with a refractometer (64°Brix), by using a thermometer (105°C/221°F) or doing the "saucer test" (see page 30).

When the density is right, add the lemon juice and flaked almonds.

Fill the jars to one centimeter from the top, seal them hermetically and place them upside down for an hour, during which they will become airtight.

After the hour has passed, immerse your jars in a tub of cold water to quickly cool the jam and preserve its color.

Dry the jars carefully and, if you like, personalize them with lettering or a label before storing them in a cool, dry place.

Mantua pumpkin jam with spices and citrus fruits

This recipe makes 3-4 250 g (9 oz) jars

Ingredients

1.5 kg (53 oz) Mantua pumpkin
castor sugar (weight equal to the weight of boiled pumpkin)
juice and zest of 1 orange
juice and zest of 1 lemon
10 cardamom pods
1 vanilla bean

Peel the pumpkin, remove the seeds and dice the flesh. Cook it for 10 minutes in boiling water, then drain and weigh it.

Put the pumpkin in a glass bowl and add an equal weight of sugar together with the orange and lemon zest, orange juice and spices.

Mix well, then cover with cling film and leave it to soak until the sugar begins to dissolve.

Put it all in a pan, place it on the hob and bring gently to the boil.

Then wait for the mixture to cool and put it in the fridge, if possible in a glass bowl. Leave it to soften in a cool place for 12 hours.

Put the pumpkin in a pan again and simmer, skimming when necessary, until the jam has reached the right density. You can check this with a refractometer (64°Brix), by using a thermometer (105°C/221°F) or doing the "saucer test" (see page 30).

When the density is right, add the lemon juice.

Fill the jars to one centimeter from the top, seal them hermetically and place them upside down for an hour, during which they will become airtight.

After the hour has passed, immerse your jars in a tub of cold water to quickly cool your jam and preserve its color.

Dry the jars carefully and, if you like, personalize them with lettering or a label before storing them in a cool, dry place.

The Mantua pumpkin or Zucca mantovana, with its sweet and unmistakable flavor, is a vegetable particularly suitable for making many sweet and savory preparations. Due to its sweetness and very intense color, it is used for delicate compotes and seasonal jams.

Ace jam
with Polignano carrots

This recipe makes 3-4 250g (9 oz) jars

Ingredients

1.3 kg (46 oz) Polignano carrots
200 ml (¾ cup) orange juice
1 kg (35 oz) sugar
zest of 1 orange
zest of 1 lemon
200 ml (¾ cup) apple juice
30 ml (⅛ cup) lemon juice

Wash the carrots well, peel them and cut them into julienne strips.

Put them in a pan, add orange juice and simmer over low heat until tender.

Put the carrots in a glass bowl, add sugar and orange and lemon zest. Mix well, then cover with cling film and leave it to soak until the sugar begins to dissolve.

Put it all in a pan, place it on the hob and bring gently to the boil.

Then wait for the mixture to cool and put it in the fridge, if possible in a glass bowl. Leave it to soften in a cool place for 12 hours.

Process everything with a blender. Put the carrots in a pan, add the apple juice and simmer, skimming when necessary, until the jam has reached the right density. You can check this with a refractometer (64°Brix), by using a thermometer (105°C/221°F) or doing the "saucer test" (see page 30).

When the density is right, add the lemon juice.

Fill the jars to one centimeter from the top, close them hermetically and place them upside down for an hour, during which they will become airtight.

After the hour has passed, immerse your jars in a tub of cold water to quickly cool your jam and preserve its color.

Dry the jars carefully and, if you like, personalize them with lettering or a label before storing them in a cool, dry place.

Polignano carrots come in various colors – yellow, orange or purple. They have a thousand hues and a very intense flavor. They are generally used in savory dishes, but are surprisingly good for making jam, as the color will always be unique and unrepeatable.

Polignano a Mare (Bari, Apulia).

Cream of chestnut with vanilla and rum

This recipe makes 3-4 250 g (9 oz) jars

Ingredients

1.5 kg (53 oz) chestnuts
800 g (28 oz) sugar
500 ml (2⅛ cups) water
30 ml (⅛ cup) rum
1 vanilla bean

Wash the chestnuts well, make a cut the with the tip of a knife along ¾ of their outer shells and simmer them in boiling water for 10 minutes.

Leave them in the water to keep them warm and remove the shell and skin underneath.

Put the chestnuts in a pan, add water, sugar and the vanilla bean cut in half and simmer, skimming when necessary, until the cream has reached the right density. You can check this with a refractometer (64°Brix), by using a thermometer (105°C/221°F) or doing the "saucer test" (see page 30).

When the density is right, add the rum and process it all in a blender until you get a smooth and velvety spread.

Fill the jars to one centimeter from the top, seal them hermetically and place them upside down for an hour, during which they will become airtight.

After the hour has passed, immerse your jars in a tub of cold water to quickly cool your jam and preserve its color.

Dry the jars carefully and, if you like, personalize them with lettering or a label before storing them in a cool, dry place.

Chestnuts are large-sized fruits with a light color and very sweet flavor. With chestnuts you can make spreads and marrons glacés, delicious sweet treats for the fall season.

Quince and cinnamon jam

This recipe makes 3-4
250 g (9 oz) jars

Ingredients
1.3 kg (46 oz) quince
zest of 1 lemon
500 ml (2⅛ cups) water
600 g (21 oz) sugar
1 cinnamon stick
60 ml (¼ cup) lemon juice

Wash the apples well and dice them, keeping the peel and core.

Remove the lemon zest with a potato peeler and cut it coarsely.

Put the fruit in a pan, add the lemon zest and water and simmer until the apples are tender. Pass everything through a vegetable mill with the medium disk and then process everything in the blender to get a smooth and velvety cream.

Put the apple pulp in a pan, add the sugar and cinnamon and simmer, skimming when necessary, until the jam has reached the right density. You can check this with a refractometer (64°Brix), by using a thermometer (105°C/221°F) or doing the "saucer test" (see page 30).

When the density is right, add the lemon juice.

Fill the jars to one centimeter from the top, seal them hermetically and place them upside down for an hour, during which they will become airtight.

After the hour has passed, immerse your jars in a tub of cold water to quickly cool your jam and preserve its color.

Dry the jars carefully and, if you like, personalize them with lettering or a label before storing them in a cool, dry place.

Late Ciaculli mandarin marmalade with spices

This recipe makes 3-4 250 g (9 oz) jars

Ingredients

750 g (26½ oz) late Ciaculli mandarins
1 kg (35 oz) sugar
1 cinnamon stick
1 star anise pod
500 ml (2⅛ cups) late Ciaculli Mandarin juice
60 ml (¼ cup) lemon juice

Wash the mandarins well and simmer them in boiling water until they become soft. Drain them, cut them into thin slices, remove the seeds and tie them in a muslin sachet.

Put the fruit in a glass bowl, add sugar, the juice of the mandarins, the sachet with the seeds, the cinnamon and the star anise pod. Mix well, then cover with cling film and leave it to soak until the sugar begins to dissolve.

Put it all in a pan, place it on the hob and bring gently to the boil. Then wait for the mixture to cool and put it in the fridge, if possible in a glass bowl. Leave it to soften in a cool place for 12 hours.

Put the fruit in a pan again and simmer, skimming as needed, until the marmalade has reached the right density. You can check this with a refractometer (64°Brix), by using a thermometer (105°C/221°F) or doing the "saucer test" (see page 30).

When the density is right, remove the sachet with the seeds and add the lemon juice.

Fill the jars to one centimeter from the top, seal them hermetically and place them upside down for an hour, during which they will become airtight.

After the hour has passed, immerse your jars in a tub of cold water to quickly cool your marmalade and preserve its color.

Dry the jars carefully and, if you like, personalize them with lettering or a label before storing them in a cool, dry place.

The late Ciaculli mandarin produces its fruits between February and April, when the mandarin season is generally over. The pulp is sweet with very few seeds, while the peel is very thin and extremely fragrant. It is a perfect fruit for making marmalade and candying.

Navel orange marmalade

This recipe makes 3-4 250 g (9 oz) jars

Ingredients

1 kg (35 oz) Navel oranges (untreated)
1 kg (35 oz) sugar
40 ml (⅛ cup) lemon juice

Wash the oranges, pierce them with a wooden toothpick and soak them in cold water for two days, changing the water twice a day.

Drain the oranges and cut them into very thin slices with a food processor. Keep the seeds and tie them in a muslin sachet.

Put the fruit in a glass bowl, add sugar and the sachet with the seeds.Mix well, then cover with cling film and leave it to soak until the sugar begins to dissolve.

Put it all in a pan, place it on the hob and bring gently to the boil. Then wait for the mixture to cool and put it in the fridge, if possible in a glass bowl. Leave it to soften in a cool place for 12 hours.

Put the fruit in a pan again and simmer, skimming as needed, until the jam has reached the right density. You can check this with a refractometer (64°Brix), by using a thermometer (105°C/221°F) or doing the "saucer test" (see page 30).

When the density is right, remove the sachet with the seeds and add the lemon juice. Fill the jars to one centimeter from the top, seal them hermetically and place them upside down for an hour, during which they will become airtight.

After the hour has passed, immerse your jars in a tub of cold water to quickly cool your marmalade and preserve its color.

Dry the jars carefully and, if you like, personalize them with lettering or a label before storing them in a cool, dry place.

Navel oranges are grown in Sicily. The name of this variety is due to the small growth, rather like a navel, found at one end of the fruit. These oranges are very fragrant and their sweet and juicy pulp is perfect for making marmalade. Thanks to their particularly thick peel, they are also ideal for candying.

Orange groves in the Ponte Barca area near Paternò (Catania, Sicily). In the background, Etna.

Bitter orange
and cinnamon marmalade

**This recipe makes 3-4
250 g (9 oz) jars**

Ingredients

**1.5 kg (53 oz) bitter
oranges (untreated)
sugar (equal in weight to
the juice from squeezing
the oranges plus the
weight of their zest)
1 cinnamon stick
30 ml (⅛ cup) lemon juice**

Wash the oranges well, cut them in half and squeeze them. Weigh the juice obtained and add the equivalent weight of sugar. Set aside the seeds and tie them in a muslin sachet.

Remove the pith from the two halves of the peel of the squeezed oranges, then slice it thinly with a food processor. Weigh the zest obtained and add the equivalent weight of sugar.

Put the zest and the juice in a glass bowl, add the sachet with the seeds and the cinnamon. Mix well, then cover with cling film and leave it to soak until the sugar begins to dissolve. Put it all in a pan, place it on the hob and bring gently to the boil. Then wait for the mixture to cool and put it in the fridge, if possible in a glass bowl. Leave it to soften in a cool place for 12 hours.

Put the fruit in a pan again and simmer, skimming as needed, until the jam has reached the right density. You can check this with a refractometer (64°Brix), by using a thermometer (105°C/221°F) or doing the "saucer test" (see page 30).

When the density is right, remove the sachet with the seeds and add the lemon juice.

Fill the jars to one centimeter from the top, seal them hermetically and place them upside down for an hour, during which they will become airtight.

After the hour has passed, immerse your jars in a tub of cold water to quickly cool your marmalade and preserve their color.

Dry the jars carefully and, if you like, personalize them with lettering or a label before storing them in a cool, dry place.

Because of their flavor, bitter oranges are hardly ever eaten raw. But they are ideal ingredients for marmalades with an unmistakable aroma and a slightly bitter taste. The essence of orange blossom (zagara) is made from their flowers.

Sicilian red orange and vanilla marmalade

This recipe makes 3-4 250 g (9 oz) jars

Ingredients

1 kg (35 oz) Sicilian red oranges (untreated), peeled and de-pithed
1.2 kg (42 oz) sugar
zest of 4 Sicilian red oranges peeled with a potato peeler
750 ml (3⅛ cups) red orange juice
2 vanilla pods
40 ml (⅛ cup) lemon juice

Cut the oranges into thin slices. Finely julienne the zest of the oranges.

Put the fruit in a glass bowl, add the sugar, zest and juice of the oranges and the vanilla pods cut in half. Mix well, then cover with cling film and leave it to soak until the sugar begins to dissolve.

Put it all in a pan, place it on the hob and bring gently to the boil. Then wait for the mixture to cool and put it in the fridge, if possible in a glass bowl. Leave it to soften in a cool place for 12 hours.

Put the fruit in a pan again and simmer, skimming as needed, until the jam has reached the right density. You can check this with a refractometer (64°Brix), by using a thermometer (105°C/221°F) or doing the "saucer test" (see page 30).

When the density is right, process your marmalade in a blender and add the lemon juice.

Fill the jars to one centimeter from the top, seal them hermetically and place them upside down for an hour, during which they will become airtight.

After the hour has passed, immerse your jars in a tub of cold water to quickly cool your marmalade and preserve its color.

Dry the jars carefully and, if you like, personalize them with lettering or a label before storing them in a cool, dry place.

The Sicilian red orange (sometimes called a blood orange) contains a natural pigment that gives it the characteristic red coloring, making it possible to obtain compotes and jams with a uniquely intense hue.

Amalfi lemon marmalade

This recipe makes 3-4 250 g (9 oz) jars

Ingredients
750 g (26½ oz) Amalfi lemons (untreated)
1.5 kg (53 oz) sugar
375 ml (1½ cups) juice of Amalfi lemons
750 ml (2⅛ cups/13 pints) apple juice

Wash the lemons well and bring them to the boil five times, always starting with cold water and changing the water each time. Cut the lemons into four parts and then into thin slices. Remove the seeds and tie them in a muslin sachet.

Put the fruit in a glass bowl, add sugar, lemon juice, apple juice and the sachet with the seeds. Mix well, then cover with cling film and leave it to soak until the sugar begins to dissolve.

Put it all in a pan, place it on the hob and bring gently to the boil. Then wait for the mixture to cool and put it in the fridge, if possible in a glass bowl. Leave it to soften in a cool place for 12 hours.

Put the fruit in a pan again and simmer, skimming as needed, until the jam has reached the right density. You can check this with a refractometer (64°Brix), by using a thermometer (105°C/221°F) or doing the "saucer test" (see page 30).

When the density is correct, remove the sachet with the seeds.

Fill the jars to one centimeter from the top, seal them hermetically and place them upside down for an hour, during which they will become airtight.

After the hour has passed, immerse your jars in a tub of cold water to quickly cool your marmalade and preserve its color.

Dry the jars carefully and, if you like, personalize them with lettering or a label before storing them in a cool, dry place.

The "Sfusato Amalfitano" lemon, from the Amalfi coast, stands out for its high concentration of essential oils. Very fragrant, juicy and with a pulp that is not too acid, it is used to make sweet liqueurs such as Limoncello and for sweet and savory marmalades. Its zest is very pulpy, excellent for candying.

Amalfi Coast (Salerno, Campania). Left: lemon trees in Val d'Elsa (Florence, Tuscany).

Clementine marmalade

This recipe makes 3-4
250 g (9 oz) jars

Ingredients
1 kg (35 oz) clementines
600 g (21 oz) sugar
200 ml (¾ cup) apple juice
20 ml lemon juice

Wash the clementines well and cut them into thin slices. Remove the seeds and tie them in a muslin sachet.

Put the fruit in a glass bowl, add the sugar and the sachet with seeds. Mix well, then cover with cling film and leave it to soak until the sugar begins to dissolve.

Put it all in a pan, place it on the hob and bring gently to the boil. Then wait for the mixture to cool and put it in the fridge, if possible in a glass bowl. Leave it to soak in a cool place for 12 hours.

Put the fruit in a pan again, add the apple juice and simmer, skimming as needed, until the jam has reached the right density. You can check this with a refractometer (64°Brix), by using a thermometer (105°C/221°F) or doing the "saucer test" (see page 30).

When the density is right, remove the sachet with the seeds and add the lemon juice, then process your marmalade in a blender.

Fill the jars to one centimeter from the top, close them hermetically and place them upside down for an hour, during which they will become airtight.

After the hour has passed, immerse your jars in a tub of cold water to quickly cool your marmalades and preserve their color.

Dry the jars carefully and, if you like, personalize them with lettering or a label before storing them in a cool, dry place.

Diamante citron marmalade

This recipe makes 3-4 250 g (9 oz) jars

Ingredients

500 g (17½ oz) Liscio di Diamante citron pulp (only the pulp of the fruit, without peel or pith)
500 g (17½ oz) Liscio di Diamante citrons (untreated)
1 kg (35 oz) sugar

Cut up the pulp of the citrons and put it in a glass bowl. Add 500 g (17½ oz) of sugar, mix well, then cover with cling film and leave it to soak until the sugar begins to dissolve.

Put it all in a pan, place it on the hob and bring gently to the boil. Then wait for the mixture to cool and put it in the fridge, if possible in a glass bowl. Leave it to soften in a cool place for 12 hours.

In the meantime, wash the whole citrons well and boil them three times for 15 minutes, always starting from cold water and changing it each time.

Cut the citrons into four parts and then slice them thinly. Remove the seeds and put them in a sachet. Put the chopped citrons, the diced pulp, the remaining sugar and the sachet with the seeds into a pan and place it on the hob. Cook everything until the fruit becomes soft. Cook, skimming when necessary, until the marmalade has reached the right density. You can check this with a refractometer (64°Brix), by using a thermometer (105°C/221°F) or doing the "saucer test" (see page 30).

When the density is right, remove the sachet and process your marmalade in a blender.

Fill the jars to one centimeter from the top, seal them hermetically and place them upside down for an hour, during which they will become airtight.

After the hour has passed, immerse your jars in a tub of cold water to quickly cool your marmalade and preserve their color.

Dry the jars carefully and, if you like, personalize them with lettering or a label before storing them in a cool, dry place.

In the Riviera dei Cedri in Calabria, they grow the citron variety 'Liscio di Diamante' (smooth Diamante), also known as "the green gold of Calabria". It is a highly prized variety, used almost exclusively in the confectionery industry for candying, making a refreshing drink and in a very delicate marmalade.

Riviera dei Cedri near Diamante. Right: smooth cedar from Santa Maria del Cedro (Cosenza, Calabria).

Compotes

You can turn all the jams and marmalades from the previous chapter into delicious compotes by decreasing the amount of sugar and using the processing technique I will explain in the following recipes. You can also use sucrose replacement sugars for compotes, taking into account their sweetening power and adapting the quantities of ingredients accordingly.

Making a compote without sugar is very simple. You just need some sweet, ripe fruit, If necessary, you can add some natural pectin and the aromas you like best.

The compotes can be stored in the refrigerator for about a week. They can be eaten like any jam or marmalade.

Personally, I have always preferred jams and marmalades, but in recent years I have greatly revised my attitude to fruit compotes: they are faster to prepare and have fewer calories. All the same, one type of preserve does not exclude the other!

The recipes:

Strawberry and cardamom compote without sugar

This recipe makes 3-4 250 g (9 oz) jars

Ingredients
1 kg (35 oz) ripe strawberries
200 ml (¾ cup) apple juice
5 cardamom pods
40 ml (⅛ cup) lemon juice

Wash the strawberries, remove the stalk, remove any damaged parts and cut the strawberries into pieces.

Put the fruit in a pan on the hob, add apple juice and cardamom. Stir well and bring to the boil. As soon as the strawberries become tender, process them with a vegetable mill.

Finish cooking, skimming as needed, until the compote reaches the desired density.

When the density is right, add the lemon juice.

Fill your jars to one centimeter from the top and seal them tightly.

To extend the storage time of your compote and avoid the growth of potentially harmful microorganisms, pasteurize the jars (see page 41).

After pasteurization, immerse your jars in a tub of cold water to quickly cool your compotes and preserve their color.

Dry the jars carefully and, if you like, personalize them with lettering or a label before storing them in a cool, dry place.

Strawberry compote with Sichuan pepper

This recipe makes 3-4
250 g (9 oz) jars

Ingredients

1 kg (35 oz) strawberries
300 g (10½ oz) sugar
grated zest of 1 lemon
a few grains of
Sichuan pepper
60 ml (¼ cup) lemon juice

Wash the strawberries, remove the stalks and any damaged parts, then cut them into pieces.

Crush the peppercorns (you can use a meat tenderizer), then put them in a muslin sachet.

Put the fruit in a pan on the hob, add sugar, the grated lemon zest and the sachet with the Sichuan pepper. Stir and bring to the boil.

As soon as the strawberries become tender, process them with a vegetable mill.

Finish cooking, skimming as needed, until the compote reaches the desired density.

When the density is right, add the lemon juice.

Fill your jars to one centimeter from the top and seal them tightly.

To extend the storage time of your compote and avoid the growth of potentially harmful microorganisms, pasteurize the jars (see page 41).

After pasteurization, immerse your jars in a tub of cold water to quickly cool your compotes and preserve their color.

Dry the jars carefully and, if you like, personalize them with lettering or a label before storing them in a cool, dry place.

Peach, amaretti and chocolate compote

This recipe makes 3-4
250 g (9 oz) jars

Ingredients
1 kg (35 oz) peaches
250 g (8¾ oz) sugar
100 g (3½ oz) dark
chocolate
50 g (1¾ oz) crumbled
amaretti cookies
30 ml (⅛ cup) rum

Wash the peaches, scald them for a minute in boiling water and leave them to cool in water and ice.

Peel them, remove the stones and any bruised parts and dice them.

Put the fruit in a pan on the hob, add the sugar and bring gently to the boil.

As soon as the peaches become tender, process them in a blender. Finish cooking, skimming as needed, until the compote reaches the desired density.

When the density is right, add the chocolate flakes, crumbled amaretti and rum.

Fill your jars to one centimeter from the top and seal them tightly.

To extend the storage time of your compote and avoid the growth of potentially harmful microorganisms, pasteurize the jars (see page 41).

After pasteurization, immerse your jars in a tub of cold water to quickly cool your compotes and preserve their color.

Dry your jars well and, if you like, personalize them with lettering or a label before storing them in a cool, dry place.

Apricot and almond compote

This recipe makes 3-4 250 g (9 oz) jars

Ingredients
1 kg (35 oz) apricots
300 g (10½ oz) sugar
grated zest of 1 lemon
30 ml (⅛ cup) lemon juice
30 ml (⅛ cup) rum
50 g (1¾ oz) toasted flaked almonds

Wash the apricots, cut them in half, remove any bruised parts as well as the stones, then dice them.

Put the fruit in a pan on the hob, add the sugar and grated lemon zest and bring to the boil.

As soon as the apricots are tender, process them in a blender.

Finish cooking, skimming as needed, until the compote reaches the desired density.

When the density is right, add the lemon juice, rum and almonds.

Fill your jars to one centimeter from the top and seal them tightly.

To extend the storage time of your compote and avoid the growth of potentially harmful microorganisms, pasteurize the jars (see page 41).

After pasteurization, immerse your jars in a tub of cold water to quickly cool your compotes and preserve their color.

Dry your jars well and, if you like, personalize them with lettering or a label before storing them in a cool, dry place.

Black fig and vanilla compote

This recipe makes 3-4 250 g (9 oz) jars

Ingredients
1 kg (35 oz) black figs
300 g (10½ oz) sugar
grated zest of 1 lemon
1 vanilla bean
60 g (2 oz) lemon juice

Wash the figs, dry them, remove the stalks and cut them into four pieces.

Put the fruit in a pan on the hob, add the sugar, the grated lemon zest, the vanilla pod cut in half and bring to the boil.

As soon as the figs become soft, remove the vanilla pod and process them with a blender.

Finish cooking, skimming as needed, until the compote reaches the desired density.

When the density is right, add the lemon juice. Fill your jars to one centimeter from the top and seal them tightly.

To extend the storage time of your compote and avoid the growth of potentially harmful microorganisms, pasteurize the jars (see page 41).

After pasteurization, immerse your jars in a tub of cold water to quickly cool your compotes and preserve their color.

Dry the jars carefully and, if you like, personalize them with lettering or a label before storing them in a cool, dry place.

Green tomato and vanilla compote

This recipe makes 3-4 250 g (9 oz) jars

Ingredients
1 kg (35 oz) green tomatoes
300 g (10½ oz) sugar
grated zest of 1 lemon
2 vanilla beans
30 ml (⅛ cup) lemon juice

Wash the tomatoes, remove the peel, any damaged parts and the seeds, then chop the tomatoes.

Put them in a pan on the hob, add sugar, the grated lemon zest, the vanilla beans cut in half and bring to the boil.

As soon as the tomatoes become soft, process them in a blender.

Finish cooking, skimming as needed, until the compote reaches the desired density.

When the density is right, add the lemon juice.

Fill your jars to one centimeter from the top and seal them tightly.

To extend the storage time of your compote and avoid the growth of potentially harmful microorganisms, pasteurize the jars.

After pasteurization, immerse your jars in a tub of cold water to quickly cool your compotes and preserve their color.

Dry the jars carefully and, if you like, personalize them with lettering or a label before storing them in a cool, dry place.

Tropea onion compote with cinnamon

This recipe makes 3-4 250 g (9 oz) jars

Ingredients

1 kg (35 oz) Tropea onions
150 g (5¼ oz) steamed beetroots
100 ml (½ cup) Moscato
50 ml (¼ cup) apple cider vinegar
50 g (1¾ oz) sultanas
350 g (12¼ oz) sugar
1 cinnamon stick

Wash the onions, remove any damaged parts and cut them into thin slices.

Separately, process the beetroots in a vegetable mill until they are pureed, then add the Moscato and apple cider vinegar.

In the meantime, wash the sultanas well, soak them for a while and then dry them carefully. Leave them aside for now.

Put everything else in a pan on the hob, add the sugar and cinnamon stick and bring to the boil.

Halfway through cooking, remove the cinnamon stick and process the compote in a blender.

Finish cooking, skimming as needed, until the compote has condensed.

When the density is right, add the sultanas.

Fill your jars to one centimeter from the top and seal them tightly.

To extend the storage time of your compote and avoid the growth of potentially harmful microorganisms, pasteurize the jars (see page 41).

After pasteurization, immerse your jars in a tub of cold water to quickly cool your compotes and preserve their color.

Dry the jars carefully and, if you like, personalize them with lettering or a label before storing them in a cool, dry place.

Church of Santa Maria dell'Isola in Tropea (Vibo Valentia, Calabria).

Apple and blueberry compote with vanilla

This recipe makes 3-4 250 g (9 oz) jars

Ingredients
800 g (28 oz) apples
300 g (10½ oz) blueberries
100 ml (½ cup) water
200 g (7 oz) sugar
2 vanilla beans
40 ml (⅛ cup) lemon juice

Wash the blueberries.

Wash the apples, peel them and cut them into thin slices. Put the seeds in a sachet.

Put the apples in a pan on the hob, add the blueberries, water, sugar, the vanilla beans cut in half and the sachet with pips and bring them gently to the boil.

As soon as the apples become soft, remove the vanilla beans and the sachet with pips and process the rest in a blender. Finish cooking, skimming as needed, until the compote reaches the desired density.

When the density is right, add the lemon juice. Fill your jars to one centimeter from the top and seal them tightly.

To extend the storage time of your compote and avoid the growth of potentially harmful microorganisms, pasteurize the jars (see page 41).

After pasteurization, immerse your jars in a tub of cold water to quickly cool your compotes and preserve their color.

Dry the jars carefully and, if you like, personalize them with lettering or a label before storing them in a cool, dry place.

Apple and peach compote with Moscato and cinnamon

This recipe makes 3-4 250 g (9 oz) jars

Ingredients
600 g (21 oz) Golden Delicious apples
600 g (21 oz) peaches
200 g (7 oz) sugar
500 ml (2⅛ cups) Moscato
2 cinnamon sticks
40 ml (⅛ cup) lemon juice

Wash the apples, peel them and cut them into thin slices. Put the seeds in a muslin sachet.

Wash the peaches, blanch them for a minute in boiling water and leave them to cool in water and ice.

Peel them, remove the stones and any bruised parts and dice them.

Put the fruit in a pan on the hob, add the sugar, Moscato, the sachet with pips and the cinnamon sticks and bring gently to the boil.

As soon as the fruit softens, remove the cinnamon sticks and the sachet with pips and process the rest in a blender. Finish cooking, skimming as needed, until the compote reaches the desired density.

When the density is right, add the lemon juice. Fill your jars to one centimeter from the top and seal them tightly.

To extend the storage time of your compote and avoid the growth of potentially harmful microorganisms, pasteurize the jars (see page 41).

After pasteurization, immerse the jars in a tub of cold water to quickly cool your compotes and preserve their color.

Dry the jars carefully and, if you like, personalize them with lettering or a label before storing them in a cool, dry place.

Pumpkin and toasted almond compote

This recipe makes 3-4 250 g (9 oz) jars

Ingredients

1.2 kg (42 oz) pumpkin
150 g (5¼ oz) sugar
grated zest of 1 lemon
30 ml (⅛ cup) lemon juice
100 g (3½ oz) toasted flaked almonds

Peel the pumpkin, remove the seeds and dice it.

Cook it in boiling water until soft.

Drain the pumpkin and put it in a pan on the hob. Add the sugar and grated lemon zest and bring gently to the boil.

As soon as the pumpkin softens, process it with a blender. Finish cooking, skimming as needed, until the compote reaches the desired density.

When the density is right, add the lemon juice and almonds.

Fill your jars to one centimeter from the top and seal them tightly.

To extend the storage time of your compote and avoid the growth of potentially harmful microorganisms, pasteurize the jars (see page 41).

After pasteurization, immerse your jars in a tub of cold water to quickly cool your compotes and preserve their color.

Dry the jars carefully and, if you like, personalize them with lettering or a label before storing them in a cool, dry place.

Almond branch (Bari, Apulia). Right: almond trees in blossom near Enna (Sicily).

Fruit jellies

Sour cherry jelly

This recipe makes 3-4 250 g (9 oz) jars

Ingredients

1 kg (35 oz) sour cherries
500 ml (2⅛ cups) apple juice
1 kg (35 oz) sugar
30 ml (⅛ cup) lemon juice

Wash your sour cherries, remove the stalks and stones.

Process the cherries with a juice extractor to obtain the juice, then filter it first through the chinoise and then through etamine fabric or sterile gauze.

Leave the juice to stand in a cool place overnight.

Then filter the juice again through the etamine fabric until it is transparent.

Weigh 500 g (17½ oz) juice and put it in a pan on the hob along with the apple juice and sugar.

Cook, skimming when necessary, until your jelly has reached the right density. You can check this by using a refractometer (70°Brix).

When the density is right, add the lemon juice.

Fill your jars to one centimeter from the top, seal them hermetically and place them upside down for an hour, during which they will become airtight.

After the hour has passed, immerse the jars in a tub of cold water to quickly cool the jelly and preserve its color.

Dry the jars carefully and, if you like, personalize them with lettering or a label before storing them in a cool, dry place.

Currant jelly

This recipe makes 3-4 250 g (9 oz) jars

Ingredients
1.2 kg (42 oz) currants
1 liter (2 pints) apple juice
1 kg (35 oz) sugar
30 ml (⅛ cup) lemon juice

Wash the currants and use a fork to remove the berries from the stems, discarding any damaged parts.

Put the currants in a pan on the hob and add the apple juice. Bring it to the boil and simmer for 15 minutes.

Filter the juice obtained first through the chinoise and then through etamine fabric or sterile gauze.

Leave the juice to stand in a cool place overnight.

Then filter the juice again using the etamine cloth until it is transparent.

Put the juice in a pan on the hob and add sugar. Cook, skimming when necessary, until the jelly has reached the right density. You can check this by using a refractometer (70°Brix).

When the density is right, add the lemon juice.

Fill the jars to one centimeter from the top, seal them hermetically and place them upside down for an hour, during which they will become airtight.

After the hour has passed, immerse the jars in a tub of cold water to quickly cool your jelly and preserve its color.

Dry the jars carefully and, if you like, personalize them with lettering or a label before storing them in a cool, dry place.

Blueberry jelly

This recipe makes 3-4
250 g (9 oz) jars

Ingredients

1 kg (35 oz blueberries
1 liter (2 pints) apple juice
1 kg (35 oz) sugar
30 ml (⅛ cup) lemon juice

Wash the blueberries and put them in a pan on the hob.

Add apple juice, bring it to the boil and simmer for 15 minutes.

Filter the juice obtained first through the chinoise and then through etamine fabric or sterile gauze.

Leave the juice to stand in a cool place overnight.

Then filter the juice again with the etamine fabric until it is transparent.

Put the juice in a pan on the hob and add the sugar. Cook, skimming when necessary, until the jelly has reached the right density. You can check this be using a refractometer (70°Brix).

When the density is right, add the lemon juice.

Fill the jars to one centimeter from the top, close them hermetically and place them upside down for an hour, during which they will become airtight.

Then immerse the jars in a tub of cold water to quickly cool your jelly and preserve its color.

Dry the jars carefully and, if you like, personalize them with lettering or a label before storing them in a cool, dry place.

Granny Smith apple and rose bud jelly

This recipe makes 3-4 250 g (9 oz) jars

Ingredients
**1.5 kg (53 oz) Granny Smith apples
1.5 liters (6½ cups) water
1 kg (35 oz) sugar
25 ml (5 teaspoons) lemon juice
dried rosebuds to taste**

Wash the apples well and cut them into four parts, removing the stalk and keep the core with the seeds.

Put the apples in a pan on the hob, add water and bring to the boil. Let it cook for about 30 minutes.

Filter the juice obtained first through the chinoise and then etamine fabric or sterile gauze.

Leave the juice to stand in a cool place overnight. Then filter the juice again through etamine fabric until it is transparent.

Put the juice in a pan on the hob and add sugar. Cook, skimming when necessary, until the jelly has reached the right density. You can check this by using a refractometer (70°Brix).

When the density is right, add the lemon juice.

Fill your jars to one centimeter from the top. Insert a few dried rosebuds into the jars to perfume your jelly. Seal the jars hermetically and place them upside down for an hour, during which they will become airtight.

Then immerse the jars in a tub of cold water to quickly cool your jelly and preserve its color.

Dry the jars carefully and, if you like, personalize them with lettering or a label before storing them in a cool, dry place.

Red apple jelly

This recipe makes 3-4 250 g (9 oz) jars

Ingredients
1 kg (35 oz) red apples
500 g (17½ oz) of peel from red apples
1.5 liters (6½ cups) apple juice
1 kg (35 oz) sugar
50 g (1¾ oz) lemon juice

Wash the apples well and cut them into four parts, removing the stalk and keep the core with the seeds.

Put the apples in a pan on the hob, add the peel and apple juice and bring to the boil. Let it cook for about 30 minutes.

Filter the juice obtained first through the chinoise and then with etamine fabric or sterile gauze.

Leave the juice to stand in a cool place overnight. Then filter the juice again through an etamine fabric until it is transparent.

Put the juice in a pan on the hob and add sugar. Cook, skimming when necessary, until the jelly has reached the right density. You can check this by using a refractometer (70°Brix).

When the density is right, add the lemon juice.

Fill your jars to one centimeter from the top, seal them and place them upside down for an hour, during which they will become airtight.

Then immerse your jars in a tub of cold water to quickly cool the jelly and preserve its color. Dry the jars carefully and, if you like, personalize them with lettering or a label before storing them in a cool, dry place.

Mandarin jelly

This recipe makes 3-4 250 g (9 oz) jars

Ingredients
500 ml (2⅛ cups) mandarin juice
500 ml (2⅛ cups) apple juice
1 kg (35 oz) sugar
juice of 2 lemons
30 ml (5 teaspoons) mandarin liqueur

Filter the juice of the mandarins first with a chinoise and then with etamine or sterile gauze.

Leave the juice to stand in a cool place overnight.

Then filter the juice again through etamine fabric until it is transparent.

Put the juice in a pan on the hob and add the apple juice and sugar. Cook, skimming when necessary, until the jelly has reached the right density. You can check this by using the refractometer (70°Brix).

When the density is right, add the lemon juice and mandarin liqueur.

Fill your jars to one centimeter from the top, seal them hermetically and place them upside down for an hour, during which they will become airtight.

After the hour has passed, immerse the jars in a tub of cold water to quickly cool the jelly and preserve its color.

Dry the jars carefully and, if you like, personalize them with lettering or a label before storing them in a cool, dry place.

Isabella grape jelly

This recipe makes 3-4 250 g (9 oz) jars

Ingredients

**1 kg (35 oz) Isabella grapes
1 liter (2 pints) apple juice
1 kg (35 oz) sugar
25 ml (5 teaspoons) lemon juice**

Remove the grapes from the stems and wash them carefully.

Put the grapes in a pan on the hob with the apple juice and bring it all to the boil. Simmer gently for about 15 minutes.

Filter the juice obtained first through the chinoise and then through etamine fabric or sterile gauze.

Leave the juice to stand in a cool place overnight.

Then filter the juice again through an etamine fabric until it is transparent.

Put the juice in a pan on the hob and add the sugar. Cook, skimming when necessary, until the jelly has reached the right density. You can check this by using a refractometer (70°Brix).

When the density is right, add the lemon juice.

Fill your jars to one centimeter from the top, seal them hermetically and place them upside down for an hour, during which they will become airtight.

Then immerse the jars in a tub of cold water to quickly cool the jelly and preserve its color.

Dry the jars carefully and, if you like, personalize them with lettering or a label before storing them in a cool, dry place.

Jelly with Moscato d'Asti and vanilla

This recipe makes 3-4
250 g (9 oz) jars

Ingredients
500 ml (2⅛ cups)
Moscato d'Asti
500 ml (2⅛ cups)
apple juice
1 vanilla bean
800 g (28 oz) sugar
25 ml (5 teaspoons)
lemon juice

Put the Moscato, the apple juice, the vanilla bean cut in half and the sugar in a pan on the hob.

Cook, skimming as needed, until the jelly has reached the right density. You can check this by using a refractometer (70°Brix).

When the density is right, add the lemon juice.

Fill your jars to one centimeter from the top, seal them hermetically and place them upside down for an hour, during which they will become airtight.

After the hour has passed, immerse the jars in a tub of cold water to quickly cool the jelly and preserve its color.

Dry the jars carefully and, if you like, personalize them with lettering or a label before storing them in a cool, dry place.

Dolcetto d'Alba jelly

This recipe makes 3-4
250 g (9 oz) jars

Ingredients

500 ml (2⅛ cups)
Dolcetto d'Alba
500 ml (2⅛ cups)
apple juice
1 kg (35 oz) sugar
25 ml (5 teaspoons)
lemon juice

Put the Dolcetto, apple juice and sugar in a pan on the hob.

Cook, skimming as needed, until the jelly has reached the right density. You can check this by using a refractometer (70°Brix).

When the density is right, add the lemon juice.

Fill your jars to one centimeter from the top, seal them hermetically and place them upside down for an hour, during which they will become airtight.

After the hour has passed, immerse your jars in a tub of cold water to quickly cool the jelly and preserve its color.

Dry the jars carefully and, if you like, personalize them with lettering or a label before storing them in a cool, dry place.

Barrels of balsamic vinegar (Modena, Emilia-Romagna). Left: Dolcetto grapes (Cuneo, Piedmont).

Jelly with balsamic vinegar of Modena

This recipe makes 3-4 250 g (9 oz) jars

Ingredients

500 ml (2⅛ cups) balsamic vinegar of Modena
500 ml (2⅛ cups) apple juice
1 kg (35 oz) sugar
25 ml (5 teaspoons) lemon juice

Put the balsamic vinegar, apple juice and sugar in a pan on the hob.

Cook, skimming as needed, until the jelly has reached the right density. You can check this by using a refractometer (70°Brix).

When the density is right, add the lemon juice.

Fill your jars to one centimeter from the top, close them hermetically and place them upside down for an hour, during which they will become airtight.

After the hour has passed, immerse your jars in a tub of cold water to quickly cool the jelly and preserve its color.

Dry the jars carefully and, if you like, personalize them with lettering or a label before storing them in a cool, dry place.

Jelly with Malvasia di Castelnuovo Don Bosco and Sichuan pepper

This recipe makes 3-4 250g (9 oz) jars

Ingredients

500 ml (2⅛ cups) Malvasia di Castelnuovo Don Bosco
500 ml (2⅛ cups) apple juice
800 (28 oz) g sugar
25 ml (5 teaspoons) lemon juice
Sichuan pepper to taste

Put the Malvasia, apple juice and sugar in a pan on the hob.

Simmer, skimming as needed, until the jelly has reached the right density. You can check this by using a refractometer (70°Brix).

When the density is right, add the lemon juice and a few Sichuan peppercorns.

Fill your jars to one centimeter from the top, seal them hermetically and place them upside down for an hour, during which they will become airtight.

After the hour has passed, immerse the jars in a tub of cold water to quickly cool the jelly and preserve its color.

Dry the jars carefully and, if you like, personalize them with lettering or a label before storing them in a cool, dry place.

Quince cheese

Ingredients

1.5 kg (53 oz) ripe quince apples
600 ml (2½ cups) water
2 large untreated lemons
sugar
bay leaves to taste

Wash the quince apples, peel them and cut them in peces. Peel the lemons with a potato peeler and squeeze them to obtain the juice (about 150 ml). Coarsely chop the zests.

Put the apples in a steel pan on the hob, add water and the juice and zest of the lemons. Simmer until the apples are soft.

Process everything first with a vegetable mill with the medium disk and then with the blender until you get a smooth and velvety puree.

Weigh the puree obtained and calculate the sugar to add, bearing in mind that for each kg of puree you need 800 g of sugar. Then put the sugar in a steel pan on the hob and add as much water as needed to cover the sugar. Cook until the sugar dissolves completely.

In the meantime, place a sheet of acetate over some steel square molds, covering the bottom and edges well.

Add the fruit puree to the sugar syrup and simmer, stirring constantly. Skim as needed, until the mixture is dry and compact. When the quince cheese has reached the right density, pour it into the square molds, level carefully and leave it to set for 48 hours.*

Then remove the frame and the acetate sheet and turn the quince cheese out onto a sheet of parchment paper. Leave it to dry well on both sides for a few days.

Cut the quince to your liking and place it in a biscuit tin. Form layers alternating the quince cheese with dried bay leaves and parchment paper. When it is time to serve, roll your quince cheese in sugar.

You can also pour the boiling quince jelly into ceramic molds previously sprinkled with lemon juice and remove them from the molds after about 8 days.

Candied fruit

Candying

Candying is a **technique for the preservation** of fruit (and, if desired, vegetables) by **simmering them in sugar syrup.**

During the candying process, the fruit releases its water content and absorbs the sugar syrup.

When two solutions of different concentration are brought into contact, they tend to balance out. The fruit loses its water to the sugar syrup, while the syrup releases sugars that penetrate the fruit.

This process, called osmosis, reaches a balance when the fruit and syrup have the same concentration.

Candying techniques

There are two candying techniques, Italian and French.

- *Italian candying* is performed with a special implement, the **candissoire**. This is a pan fitted with a small tap, which allows the syrup to be run off without touching the fruit.

  If you have a *candissoire*, each day you will have to open the tap and let the syrup run out, which you will then bring to the boil in a separate pan. After that, you will need to pour the syrup back over the fruit in the *candissoire*.

  In this way, the sugar concentration of the syrup increases by about 3-4°Brix each day. Indicatively, it takes **between 7 and 10 days** to reach the sugar concentration of **70°Brix**, depending on various factors: the type of fruit, its degree of ripeness, and the size of the pieces used.

  In the absence of a *candissoire* with a tap, you can use an ordinary steel pan. In this case, you will need to gently pour the syrup into another pan each day, bring it to the boil and pour it over the fruit again.

  I advise you to always put some kitchen mesh over the fruit, so as to always keep it immersed in the syrup for the whole candying period.

- *French candying* (also called the **"heat technique"**) consists of putting the fruit covered with boiling sugar syrup in an electric *candissoire* with controlled temperature. The fruit, completely immersed in the syrup, is kept at a **constant temperature of 50-60°C (120-140°F)** until it reaches 70°Brix.

  With this technique, the candying process is greatly accelerated.

  If you do not have an electric *candissoire*, you can use a kitchen dessicator or the oven, setting the temperature at 50-60°C (120-140°F) and keeping it constant until it reaches 70°Brix.

Suggestions and hints

Regardless of the candying technique you choose to use, I would like to offer some suggestions and advice.

- In my recipes I have chosen to candy the fruit following the **Italian technique**. I did it for the sake of practicality and because I don't need to candy **large quantities of fruit in a short time**.

- The procedure is the same for all recipes. The changes only concern some **methods for preparing the fruit** depending on their **form, size, pulp** or whether or not they are particularly rich in water and how delicate they are.

- I am often asked if candying can be done with all types of fruit and vegetables. In theory, yes, there are no limits. Any vegetable could be candied. Personally, however, I tend to almost exclusively candy citrus fruits and a few others.

- Pricking fresh fruit or freezing it are two ways to achieve the same goal: **breaking the pulp down** to favor both the loss of water and the penetration by the sugar syrup. In some cases, you will have to use both steps, as some fruit retains its shape better if it is first pricked and then frozen before the candying process.

- When 70°Brix is reached, a certain percentage of **glucose syrup** is added to the syrup to avoid crystallizing the candying syrup. Only in some cases is glucose syrup added at the start and not at the end. This happens, for example, with particularly delicate or very water-rich fruits. Glucose syrup, in addition to having an anti-crystallizing power, also has the ability to modify the texture and viscosity of the fruit. These variations, however small, will make all the difference to your finished product.

- As you will see in the recipes, my advice is to **always prepare a generous dose of syrup**, to avoid not having enough to completely cover the fruit. If you have some syrup left over, you can use it to sweeten aperitifs and herb teas.

- As in cooking and pastry, there are different schools of thought also about candying. Always remember that any method that produces an excellent result is an excellent method!

Candied orange zest

Ingredients

2 kg (70 oz) untreated Navel oranges with thick peel

For the syrup

2 liters (8½ cups) water
2 kg (70 oz) sugar
glucose syrup

Wash the oranges well. Use a long toothpick to prick them deeply in several places, then cut them into fours and remove the zest. You will need to get 1 kg (35 oz) of zest. Soak the zest in cold water and leave it there for 48 hours, changing the water at least twice a day.

Then drain the zest and put it in a pan on the hob. Add water to cover the zest and simmer until slightly soft. Use a toothpick to check its softness. When the zest is soft enough, drain it gently.

Separately, make the syrup by simmering the water and sugar for 15 minutes, skimming as needed. Turn off the cooker, add the peel and leave it to soak in the syrup for 24 hours.

The next day, pour the syrup into another pan and put it on a stove. Simmer it for 5 minutes, skimming when necessary to keep the syrup clear. Turn off the cooker, add the orange zest and leave it to soak in the syrup for another 24 hours.

Repeat the same operation every day, increasing the Brix by about 3-4 degrees per day.

When it reaches 70°Brix, gently remove the zest from the syrup and arrange it neatly in your previously sterilized jars. Weigh the syrup needed to cover the zest and add 30% of its weight in glucose syrup. Bring everything to the boil and let it boil for 5 minutes, skimming well to keep the syrup clear. Pour the boiling syrup into the jars until the zest is completely covered, then seal tightly.

Pasteurize your jars in boiling water for a variable time depending on the capacity of the jar (see page 41). In general, for 1 kg (35 oz) jars it will take 40 minutes.

Then immerse the jars in a tub of cold water to quickly lower the temperature. Dry the jars carefully and, if you like, personalize them with lettering or a label before storing them in a cool, dry place.

Candied sour cherries

Ingredients
1 kg (35 oz) sour cherries

For the syrup
1.5 liters (6½ cups) water
1.5 kg (53 oz) sugar
glucose syrup

Wash the sour cherries well and remove the stalks and stones. Arrange the cherries on a baking tin previously lined with parchment paper and place them in the freezer for 24 hours.

The next day, place the frozen cherries in a pan filled with water and let them thaw.

Separately, make the syrup by boiling the water and sugar for 15 minutes, skimming as needed. Turn off the heat, add the cherries and leave them to soak in the syrup for 24 hours.

The next day, pour the syrup into another pan and place it on the hob. Let it boil for 5 minutes, skimming when necessary, to keep the syrup clear. Turn off the cooker, add the cherries and let them soak in the syrup for another 24 hours.

Repeat the same operation every day considering increasing the brix by about 3-4 degrees per day.

When the mixture reaches (70°Brix), gently remove the cherries from the syrup and arrange them neatly in the previously sterilized jars.

Weigh the syrup needed to cover the cherries and add 30% of its weight in glucose syrup. Bring everything to the boil and simmer it for 5 minutes, skimming well to keep the syrup clear. Pour the boiling syrup into the jars until the cherries are completely covered, then seal tightly.

Pasteurize the jars in boiling water for a variable time depending on the capacity of the jar (see page 41). Generally, it takes 40 minutes for 1 kg (35 oz) jars.

After the time has passed, immerse the jars in a tub of cold water to cool them quickly. Dry the jars carefully and, if you like, personalize them with lettering or a label before storing them in a cool, dry place.

Candied kumquat

Ingredients
2 kg (70 oz) kumquats

For the syrup
3 liters (12 cups) water
3 kg (105 oz) sugar
glucose syrup

Wash the kumquats well, pierce them with a long toothpick and place them in a pan in the freezer for 24 hours.

Place the frozen kumquats in a pot full of water and let them thaw. Bring the water to the boil and leave the kumquats to cook for 5-10 minutes until they are soft, by touching them with a toothpick. When they are soft enough, drain them gently.

Separately, make the syrup by boiling the water and sugar for 15 minutes, skimming as needed. Turn off the cooker, add the kumquats and let them soak in the syrup for 24 hours.

The next day, pour the syrup into another pan and put it on the stove. Let it boil for 5 minutes, skimming when necessary to keep the syrup clear. Turn off the heat, add the kumquats and let them soak in the syrup for another 24 hours.

Repeat the same operation every day considering increasing the brix by about 3-4 degrees per day.

When the syrup reaches 70°Brix, gently remove the kumquats from the syrup and arrange them neatly in your previously sterilized jars. Weigh the syrup needed to cover the kumquats and add 30% of its weight in glucose syrup.

Bring everything to the boil and simmer for 5 minutes, skimming well to keep the syrup clear. Pour the boiling syrup into the jars until the kumquats are completely covered, then seal tightly.

Pasteurize the jars in boiling water for a variable time depending on the capacity of the jar (see page 41). Generally, it takes 40 minutes for 1 kg (35 oz) jars.

After the time has passed, immerse the jars in a tub of cold water to quickly lower the temperature. Dry the jars carefully and, if you like, personalize them with lettering or a label before storing them in a cool, dry place.

Candied mandarins

Ingredients

1 kg (35 oz) firm mandarins

For the syrup

1.5 liters (6½ cups) water
1.5 kg (53 oz) sugar
300 g (10½ oz) glucose syrup

Wash the tangerines well, remove the two ends and cut them into slices ½ cm thick. Check that all the slices are perfectly intact and compact.

Arrange them in layers on a baking sheet, alternating the slices with sheets of parchment paper, taking care to keep the slices separate from each other, then put them in the freezer overnight.

Place the frozen mandarin slices in a pan full of water and let them thaw. Bring the water to the boil and simmer the mandarin slices for 5-10 minutes, then drain them gently.

Pour the water, sugar and glucose syrup into a large pan, place it on the hob and bring to the boil. When the syrup boils, carefully immerse the mandarin slices and simmer them gently for 10 minutes. Turn off the cooker and let the mandarins cool in the syrup for 24 hours.

The next day, gently heat the fruit and syrup until it reaches 60°C (140°F), then turn off the cooker and let it cool.

Repeat this process several times during the day, trying to keep the temperature constant at 60°C (140°F).

Let the mandarins cool in the syrup overnight.

Repeat this process every day, until the syrup reaches 70°Brix.

When the density is right, gently remove the mandarin slices from the syrup and arrange them neatly in your previously sterilized jars.

Bring the syrup to the boil and let it boil for 5 minutes, skimming well to keep it clear.

Pour the boiling syrup into the jars until the mandarins are completely covered, then seal tightly.

Pasteurize the jars in boiling water for a variable time depending on the capacity of the jar (see page 41). Generally, it takes 40 minutes for 1 kg (35 oz) jars.

Then immerse the jars in a tub of cold water to quickly lower the temperature.

Dry the jars carefully and, if you like, personalize them with lettering or a label before storing them in a cool, dry place.

For this recipe I used a mixed candying technique, partly Italian and partly French, the result of an insight I had while trying to figure out how to solve some practical problems.

Sliced mandarin is extremely delicate. Also, I don't have a temperature controlled candissoire or a dessicator. To avoid keeping the oven on day and night, I decided to keep the daytime temperature of the pan containing the syrup and fruit fairly constant. This process only takes a few minutes to turn on the gas cooker from time to time. Nothing else.

I have tested this technique several times: the result is extraordinary! The slices remain intact and the candying process becomes much faster. In a few days, 70°Brix is reached without even the need to skim because, by not bringing the syrup to the boil, it always remains transparent and limpid.

Candied apricots

For this preparation it is important for the apricots to be perfectly healthy, not fully ripe and firm.

Ingredients
1.5 kg (53 oz) of apricots

For the syrup
2 liters (8½ cups) water
2 kg (70 oz) sugar
400 g (14 oz) glucose syrup

Wash the apricots well, cut them in half and remove the stone. Pierce them with a toothpick and place them in a baking tin, layering them on sheets of parchment paper and keep them in the freezer compartment for 24 hours.

Pour the water, sugar and glucose syrup into a large pan, bring to the boil and simmer for 15 minutes, skimming when necessary. Allow the frozen apricots to warm, remove from the hob and leave them immersed in the syrup overnight.

The next day, gently heat the fruit and syrup until it reaches 60°C (140°F), then turn off the heat and let it cool.

Repeat this process several times during the day, trying to keep the temperature constant at 60°C (140°F).

Let the apricots cool in the syrup overnight. Repeat this process every day, until the syrup reaches 70°Brix. When the density is right, gently remove the apricots from the syrup and arrange neatly in the previously sterilized jars.

Bring the syrup to a boil and simmer it for 5 minutes, skimming carefully to make sure it is always clear. Pour the boiling syrup into the jars until the apricots are completely covered, then close tightly.

Pasteurize the jars in boiling water for a time that will vary depending on the size of the jar (see page 41). It generally takes 40 minutes for 1 kg (35 oz) jars.

Then immerse the pots in a tub of cold water to quickly lower the temperature. Carefully wipe the jars dry and, if you like, personalize them with an inscription or label before storing them in a cool, dry place.

Candied oranges

For this preparation, it is important for the oranges to be small (about 100 g/3½ oz each), very compact and firm. The peel must be thin.

Ingredients

1.5 kg (53 oz) untreated Tarocco oranges

For the syrup

2 liters (8½ cups) water
2 kg (70 oz) sugar
400 g (14 oz) glucose syrup

Wash the oranges well, slice off either end and cut them into ½ cm thick slices. Check that all the slices are perfectly intact and compact.

Arrange them in layers on a baking sheet, alternating the slices with sheets of parchment paper, taking care to keep the slices well separate from each other, then place them in the freezer for 24 hours.

Put the frozen orange slices in a pot full water and let them thaw. Bring the water to the boil and let the orange slices cook for 5-10 minutes, then drain them gently.

Pour the water, sugar and glucose syrup into another large pan, place it on the hob and bring to the boil.

When the syrup boils, carefully immerse the orange slices and simmer them gently for 15 minutes. Turn off the cooker and let the oranges cool in the syrup for 24 hours.

The next day, pour the syrup into another pan and place it on the hob. Let it boil for 5 minutes, skimming when necessary to keep the syrup clear.

Turn off the heat, add the orange slices and let them soak in the syrup for another 24 hours.

Repeat the same operation every day considering increasing the brix by about 3-4 degrees per day.

When the syrup reaches (70°Brix), gently remove the orange slices and arrange them neatly in your previously sterilized jars. Bring the syrup to the boil and let it boil for 5 minutes, skimming well, until it becomes clear. Pour the boiling syrup into the jars until the peel is completely covered, then seal tightly.

Pasteurize the jars in boiling water for a variable time depending on the capacity of the jar (see page 41). Indicatively, it takes 40 minutes for 1 kg (35 oz) jars.

Then immerse the jars in a tub of cold water to quickly lower the temperature.

Dry the jars carefully and, if you like, personalize them with lettering or a label before storing them in a cool, dry place.

Candied grapefruit

Ingredients
4 pink grapefruits

For the syrup
2 liters (8½ cups) water
2 kg (70 oz) sugar
a second batch of
2 kg (70 oz) sugar

Wash the grapefruits well. Put them in a pan on the hob, add water until the fruit is completely covered and bring to the boil. Let the grapefruits cook for 10 minutes.

Separately, make the syrup by boiling the water and 2 kg (70 oz) of sugar for 15 minutes, skimming as needed.

Cut the grapefruits in half and dip them in the syrup. Lower the heat and let them simmer gently for 30 minutes. Let the grapefruits soak in the syrup for 24 hours.

The next day, pour the syrup into another pan, place it on the hob and add 500 g (17½ oz) sugar. Let it boil for 5 minutes, skimming when necessary, to keep the syrup clear.

Turn off the cooker, add the grapefruits and let them soak in the syrup for another 24 hours.

Repeat the same operation for another 3 days, adding 500 g (17½ oz) sugar at a time.

Then, gently remove the grapefruits from the syrup, cut them into 4 and arrange the slices neatly in the previously sterilized jars.

Pour the boiling syrup into the jars until the grapefruit slices are completely covered, then seal tightly.

Given the high percentage of sugar in this recipe, there is no need to pasteurize the jars.

I only use this procedure for grapefruit. It is a very fast candying process, given the high quantity of sugar used. In this case, I candy the whole grapefruit with all the pulp and I serve it cut into thick slices as a pre-dessert or cut thinner, for decorations in plated desserts.

Candied citron zest

Ingredients

1.5 kg (53 oz) **Diamante citrons**

For the syrup

2 liters (8½ cups) **water**
2 kg (70 oz) **sugar**
glucose syrup

Wash the citrons well, cut them into 4 segments and remove the central pulp. You will need to get 1 kg (35 oz) of peel. Put the peel with the pith in a pan, then place them in the freezer for 24 hours.

Put the frozen peel in a pot full water and let it thaw. Bring the water to the boil and leave the peel to cook for about 30 minutes until you can tell they are soft by poking them with a toothpick. When they are soft enough, drain them gently.

Separately, make the syrup by boiling the water and sugar for 15 minutes, skimming as needed. Turn off the heat, add the citron peel and let it soak in the syrup for 24 hours.

The next day, pour the syrup into another pan and place it on the hob. Let it boil for 5 minutes, skimming when necessary to keep the syrup clear. Turn off the heat, add the peel and leave it to soak in the syrup for another 24 hours.

Repeat the same operation every day, increasing the Brix by about 3-4 degrees per day.

When the syrup reaches 70°Brix, gently remove the peel and arrange it neatly in the previously sterilized jars.

Weigh the syrup needed to cover the peel and add 30% of its weight in glucose syrup. Bring everything to the boil and simmer for 5 minutes, skimming well to keep the syrup clear.

Pour the boiling syrup into the jars until the peel is completely covered, then seal tightly. Pasteurize the jars in boiling water for a variable time depending on the capacity of the jar (see pag 41). Generally, it takes 40 minutes for 1 kg (35 oz) jars.

After the time has passed, immerse the jars in a tub of cold water to quickly lower the temperature. Dry the jars carefully and, if you like, personalize them with lettering or a label before storing them in a cool, dry place.

How to use any leftover sugar syrup

In the recipes to make candied fruit I have always calculated **a quantity of syrup higher than the quantity usually needed.** This is to prevent the syrup from being insufficient during the candying process, with the risk of the sugar crystallizing on the fruit. This can be caused by various factors: the use of a pot of the wrong size, the quantity of fruit to be candied, a too lively flame or overboiling the syrup, so causing the water to evaporate.

So it can happen that, after candying, some syrup is left over. To avoid waste, I thought of ways to use the extra syrup as a **sweetener in other recipes.**

The first recipe I suggest is orange paste, to be used to perfume your desserts (tarts and pies, cookies, cakes or sweet leavened products).

Another way to use your extra candied syrup is the result of a recent intuition of mine. I'm particularly proud of it because, as far as I know, it's a technique that has never been used.

You can make excellent fruit compotes using candied syrup instead of sugar! As always, you can adjust the sweetness of the final product according to your personal taste. Keep in mind that, indicatively, **1 liter (2 pints) of syrup at 70°Brix corresponds to 700 g (24½ oz) sugar and 300 g (10½ oz) water.**

Another point in favor of this technique is that by adding the sugar in the form of syrup, the cooking of compotes is accelerated, as the fruit absorbs it more easily.

You never stop being surprised and learning in the kitchen. Just let your imagination range!

Candied orange paste

Ingredients

candied orange zest
(see page 157)
candying syrup of the zest

Put the candied orange zest in a food processor, add the candied syrup and process the zest until you get a smooth, even paste with a creamy consistency.

I recommend that you keep the candied orange paste in small, hermetically sealed jars.

If you want to keep it for longer, pasteurize the jars in boiling water for a variable time depending on their capacity (see pag 41). Generally, it takes 20 minutes for 250g (9 oz) jars.

After pasteurization, immerse the jars in a tub of cold water to quickly lower the temperature. Dry the jars carefully and, if you like, personalize them with lettering or a label before storing them in a cool, dry place.

Orange compote

This recipe will make about 3-4 250g (9 oz) jars

Ingredients

1 kg (35 oz) oranges
400 g (14 oz) sugar syrup at 70°Brix
30 ml (⅛ cup) lemon juice

Wash the oranges, pierce them with a wooden toothpick and soak them in cold water for two days, changing the water twice a day.

Drain the oranges, cut them into four parts, remove the seeds and cut the oranges into very thin slices with a food processor.

Put them in a pan on the hob, add the sugar syrup and simmer the compote.

As soon as the oranges become tender, process them in a blender. Finish cooking, skimming as needed, until the compote reaches the desired density.

When the density is right, add the lemon juice.

Fill the jars to one centimeter from the top and seal them tightly.

To extend the storage time of your compote and avoid the growth of potentially harmful microorganisms, pasteurize the jars (see page 41). Generally, it will take 20 minutes for 250 g (9 oz) jars.

After pasteurization, immerse your jars in a tub of cold water to quickly cool your compotes and preserve their color.

Dry the jars carefully and, if you like, personalize them with lettering or a label before storing them in a cool, dry place.

Other specialties

"Four colors" loaf of bread

Use a rectangular bread loaf pan, with a lid, measuring about 30x10 cm (12x4 in)

Ingredients
875 g (31 oz) type 1 flour
450 ml (1 ¾ cup) whole milk
15 g (½ oz) compressed yeast
22 g (¾ oz) granulated sugar
17 g (½ oz) salt
85 g (3 oz) lard
mixed oil seeds
(sesame, flax, poppy, chia, pumkin, sunflower)

For the "green" dough
10 g (⅓ oz) of Matcha tea brewed in
15 ml (½ oz) water

For the "brown" dough
10 g (⅓ oz) of unsweetened cocoa powder brewed in
15 ml (½ oz) water

For the "pink" dough
the contents of a sachet of hibiscus tea brewed in
20 ml (½ oz) hot water

Pour the flour into the mixer bowl, add the milk and mix well.

Cover with cling film and let it rest for an hour.

Add the yeast. Wait for a few minutes and first add the sugar, second the salt and third the lard. The dough must be elastic but firm. When the right firmness is reached, weigh the dough and divide it into 4 equal parts.

Add the Matcha tea to one part, the cocoa to another part and the hibiscus tea to a third. The fourth part of the dough will remain natural.

Cover the dough and let it rest for 20 minutes. Divide each block into 5 parts and form a ball with each.

Place the dough in a greased bread loaf tin, alternating the colored doughs. Press them down well to fill the whole tin.

Brush its surface with water, and make the oil seeds stick well.

Close the lid of the bread loaf tin but leaving a small slot open: you will need it to check how the dough rises.

Cover the mold with a nylon cloth and let the dough rise to the edge.

When the dough has risen sufficiently, close the lid and bake at 200°C (390°F) in a ventilated oven for about 1 hour.

This type of bread is perfect for breakfast.
Type 1 flour, rich in fiber and nutrients, gives the bread a rustic and genuine look. The tightly woven crumb is ideal for toasting and as a base for jams and marmalades. The "green" dough is flavored with Matcha tea, the "brown" dough with cocoa and the "pink" dough with hibiscus tea. Each variant has a unique color and aroma!

Braided loaf with seeds

Use a bread mold measuring about 30x10 cm (12x4 in)

Ingredients
600 g (21 oz) type 1 flour
400 g (14 oz) re-milled whole durum wheat semolina
500 ml (2⅛ cups) whole milk
15 g (½ oz) compressed yeast
25 g (2 tablespoons) granulated sugar
20 g (1½ tablespoons) salt
120 g (4¼ oz) butter
mixed oil seeds
(sesame, flax, poppy, chia, pumpkin, sunflower)

In the bowl of the planetary mixer, mix the two kinds of flour with the milk, then cover with cling film and let it rest for an hour.

Then start making the dough by adding the yeast. After a few minutes add the sugar, salt and softened butter.

Let the dough rest for 1 hour at room temperature.

Then shape a loaf, cover it with cling film and put it in the refrigerator for 12 hours.

Weigh the dough, divide it into three parts and with each of these create a slightly elongated loaf. Cover everything with cling film and let it rest for 10 minutes.

Make the loaves of dough as long as the mold of your choice. Brush them with a little water, press them in the mixed seeds and braid them.

Grease the mold with extra virgin olive oil and sprinkle it with seeds, then place the braided loaf in it.

Cover the mold with cling film and let the dough rise until it doubles in size.

Bake the braided loaf at 200°C (390°F) in a ventilated oven for about 1 hour.

This seeded braided loaf is very soft and fragrant, ideal for breakfast, and excellent to serve with an assortment of jams and marmalades.

Jam or marmalade tart

**Recipe for
2 tarts measuring
18 cm (7 in) across**

Ingredients

500 g (17 ½ oz) 180W flour
*(180W is a flour strength
indicator)*
300 g (10½ oz) butter
200 g (7 oz) icing sugar
80 g (3 oz) egg yolks
*(corresponding to about 5
medium-sized egg yolks)*
grated zest of 1 lemon
1 vanilla bean

For the filling

jam or marmalade
of your choice

In a mixer with the K beater, mix the flour and butter. Add the sugar, egg yolks and flavorings. Form the dough into a loaf, cover it with cling film and let it cool well in the refrigerator before using it.

Always knead the short-crust pastry a little before rolling it out. This will help keep it from breaking.

Roll out the dough with a rolling pin on a table lightly sprinkled with flour, then use it to line the bottom of a buttered mold.

Pierce the bottom of the dough well with the prongs of a fork and spread the chosen jam evenly up to 1 cm (less than ½ inch) from the edge of the mold.

Create strips of short-crust pastry and arrange them in a grid over the jam.

Roll out the chilled dough remaining on a sheet of parchment paper or Silpat baking mat. Cut a disk of the same diameter as the tart, then cut out the center leaving only a ring about 2 cm (less then ½ inch) wide. Leave the dough ring in the refrigerator for about half an hour, then place it on top of the tart, around the circumference. In this way you will get a perfect edge!

Bake the tart at 180°C (356°F) in a fan oven for about 25-30 minutes.

Citrus fruit brioches

This recipe will make about 40 brioches

Ingredients

1 kg (35 oz) 300W flour *(300W is a flour strength indicator)*
300 g (10½ oz) butter
200 ml (¾ cup) whole milk
20 g (1½ tablespoons) compressed yeast
300 g (10½ oz) eggs *(about 5½ medium-sized eggs)*
200 g (7 oz) sugar
20 g (1½ tablespoons) salt
grated zest of 1 lemon, 1 orange and 1 lime
20 g (1½ tablespoons) orange paste (see page 167)

To brush

1 whole egg and 1 yolk

For the finishing

sugar pearls or icing sugar
orange marmalade
(see page 91)

Start making the dough with the flour, milk, yeast and eggs. Little by little, add sugar, salt, citrus fruit zest, orange paste and soft butter in this order.

Let the dough rest for an hour at room temperature, then form a loaf, cover it with cling film and refrigerate it for 12 hours.

Divide the cold dough into portions of 50 g (1¾ oz) each, then shape into balls and place them in baking cups with the seam at the bottom.

Lightly brush with the egg, sprinkle with the sugar pearls, cover with a nylon cloth and let the dough rise until it doubles in size.

Bake at 190°C/375°F in a ventilated oven for about 15 minutes.

Allow them to cool, then cut them in half and stuff them with orange marmalade. Before serving, sprinkle them with powdered sugar.

Strawberry heart madeleines

Ingredients

375 g (13 oz) butter
270 g (9½ oz) eggs
(corresponding to about 5 medium-sized eggs)
240 g (8½ oz) sugar
60 g (2 oz) acacia honey
110 ml (½ cup) whole milk
375 g (13 oz) 180W flour
(180W is an indicator of the strength of the flour)
18 g (½ oz) yeast
grated zest of 2 lemons

For the filling
strawberry jam

For the finishing
icing sugar

Melt the butter and then let it cool again until it reaches room temperature.

In a glass bowl, whisk the eggs, sugar, honey and milk. Add the flour and baking powder sifted together, the butter at room temperature and, lastly, the grated lemon zest.

Cover the dough with kitchen cling film and let it rest in the refrigerator overnight.

Butter and flour a madeleine mold, place a little batter in each mold and fill with the strawberry jam. Cover the jam with the batter and refrigerate for 1 hour.

Then, bake at 200°C (390°F) for 5-6 minutes.

When you take the madeleines out of the oven, immediately remove them from the mold and leave them to cool on a sheet of parchment paper or Silpat baking mat. Before serving, sprinkle the madeleines with a little icing sugar.

Ovis mollis

Ingredients

200 g (7 oz) butter
100 g (3½ oz) icing sugar
100 g (3½ oz) of
hard-boiled egg yolks
*(corresponding to
about 6 medium-sized
egg yolks)*
200 g (7 oz) 180W flour
*(180W is the indication of
the strength of the flour)*
100 g (3½ oz)
potato starch
grated zest of 1 lemon
1 vanilla bean

For the finishing
icing sugar

Also
assorted jams to taste

Mix the soft butter well in a mixer with a K beater. Add the icing sugar, the hard-boiled yolks processed through a sieve, the sifted flour and starch together, the grated lemon zest and the vanilla.

Form a loaf and cover it with cling film. Let the dough cool well in the refrigerator before using it.

Always knead the dough a little before rolling it out with a rolling pin. This will prevent it from breaking.

Roll out the dough with a rolling pin and cut it out into an even number of small disks of the size you prefer.

Cut off half of these in the center with a smaller pastry ring, so creating dough rings.

Arrange the disks on a sheet of parchment paper or Silpat baking mat and cover them with a thin layer of jam. Finally, place the pastry ring on top of the other disk, along the circumference.

Bake at 160°C (320°F) and in a ventilated oven for about 12-13 minutes.

When they are cooked, allow the cookies to cool and lightly stuff the center of each with some more jam. In this way, they will look fresher. Before serving, sprinkle the cookies with icing sugar.

Ovis mollis is a biscuit made of short-crust pastry that has a special ingredient, the yolk of a hard-boiled egg which, kneaded together with flour, butter and sugar, makes the dough particularly delicate and crumbly, perfect for making plain or filled shortbread cookies.

Honey rusks

Recipe for 4 bread molds measuring about 20 cm (8 inches)

Ingredients for the "biga" (pre-dough)
170 g (6 oz) type 1 flour
75 ml (⅓ cup) water
2 g (¾ teaspoon) compressed yeast

Ingredients for the dough
1 kg (35 oz) type 1 flour
400 ml (1⅔ cups) milk
the whole "biga" previously prepared
80 g (3 oz) eggs (equivalent to about 1 and a half medium-sized eggs)
10 g (3½ teaspoons) compressed yeast
200 g (7 oz) sugar
60 g (2 oz) acacia honey
12 g (¾ oz) salt
100 g (3½ oz) butter
icing sugar

In addition:
assorted jams and marmalades to taste

Mix all the ingredients for the biga and knead it quickly. Let it ferment for 18-20 hours at a temperature of 18°C (65°F) degrees.

Start the dough with flour, milk, biga, eggs and yeast. After a few minutes add sugar and honey, then salt and, lastly, the softened butter.

Cover the dough with cling film and let it rest for 30 minutes at room temperature.

Cut the dough into pieces of 400g (14 oz) each.

Shape into slightly elongated loaves, then place them in previously buttered 20 cm (8 inches) long cake molds. Cover the molds with a nylon cloth and place them in the refrigerator for 12 hours.

After the 12 hours have passed, take the molds out of the refrigerator and let them rest at room temperature for about an hour or an hour and a half.

Bake at 170°C (340°F) in a ventilated oven for about 30 minutes. After cooking, take them out and leave them to cool.

The next day, cut the loaves into slices, sprinkle them with icing sugar and lightly toast them in the oven at 160°C (320°F).

Elderflower syrup

This recipe will make about 1 liter (2 pints) of elderberry syrup

Ingredients
750 ml (3⅛ oz) water
1.5 kg (53 oz) sugar
100 g (3½ oz) elderflowers
2 oranges (untreated)
2 lemons (untreated)
2 vanilla pods

Pour the water and sugar into a pan, place it on the hob and bring to the boil until you get a syrup.

Let the syrup boil for a few minutes, skimming well to keep it clear, then let it cool.

Cut the stems of the elder flowers and shake them gently to get rid of any remaining insects after harvesting. Quickly wash the flowers in cold water and then place them to dry on a linen or cotton tea towel.

Wash and dry the oranges and lemons carefully, remove the two ends and cut everything into thin slices, keeping the zest.

Put the flowers, the vanilla pods cut in half, and the slices of oranges and lemon in a big bowl then pour the sugar syrup over them. Seal the jar with kitchen cling film, making small holes in it with a needle. Leave the mixture to soak for three days in the sun, gently shaking the jar a couple of times a day.

After three days, filter the syrup through etamine fabric until it is clear of impurities. Fill the jars and seal them tightly.

Pasteurize the jars in boiling water (see page 41) for a variable time depending on the capacity of the jar. As a rough guide, a ½ liter (1 pint) jar will take 30 minutes.

After pasteurization, immerse the jars in a tub of cold water to quickly lower the temperature. Dry the jars carefully and, if you like, personalize them with lettering or a label before storing them in a cool, dry place.

I couldn't finish this book without giving you my elderberry syrup recipe. You will need the flowers of the elderberry bush, recognizable because they resemble many small white sweet-smelling stars, which bloom in late spring. You can use this fragrant syrup to sweeten your drinks or create excellent cocktails.

Thanks

I wish to thank my daughter, the impartial judge of my experiments, for encouraging me to write this book. My parents: I owe my passion for cooking to them. My husband, because he still gets excited when I get something right.

Thanks to my friends Francesca, Donatella and Nicoletta for sharing their passion for cooking and pastry with me every day.

Special thanks to Giovanni Simeone, for believing in me and in my project despite the difficulties of the pandemic. To Marco Arduino and his wife Eleonora, for making this book even more delicious with their photographs.

To Elena Pecchioli of the Fattoria di Camporomano, for hosting our photo shoot in her home.

To all the Chefs who have transmitted their knowledge to me over the years, my greatest thanks go to them.

To Stefano Laghi and Alexandre Bourdeaux, the greatest admirers and consumers of my orange marmalades.

To all the participants of the iCook Academy, for making the bread and jam snacks special.

Finally, to all you who, despite the long wait, have desired this book almost as much as I have. And to you, who will allow me to enter your kitchens... Thank you!

Francesca

Index of recipes

2022 © SIME BOOKS

Text
Francesca Maggio
Editor
Anna Martinelli
Photo Editor
Giovanni Simeone
Design
Jenny Biffis
Prepress
Fabio Mascanzoni

All the photos were taken byi **Marco Arduino** except for:
Stefano Amantini p. 102 - Franco Cogoli p. 23 - Marco Cristofori p. 62 - Colin Dutton p.122,
p. 139 - Susy Mezzanotte p. 74 - Joe Murador p. 11 - Arcangelo Piai p. 103 - Daniele Ravenna
p.66 - Massimo Ripani p.138 - Alessandro Saffo p.92-93, p.123, 190-191 - Simeone Giovanni
p. 2-3, p. 99, 116-117 - Laurent Grandadam p. 10 - Andreas Vitting p.75

Photos available on **www.simephoto.com**

First Edition: October 2022
ISBN: 978-88-31403-18-4

SIME BOOKS
www.simebooks.com